On the Cover:

The cover photo was submitted by Crista Hawkins of Beaverton, Oregon.

"OUR SON Steffan enjoyed playing in the mud puddles and roaming among the flowers on our trip to a tulip farm," says Crista. "As I took this picture, he was running toward me squealing with delight, as if to say, 'Isn't the world a great place, Mommy?'"

Contents

Editor:
Lorry Erickson

Associate Editors:
Susan Uphill, Paula Wiebel,
Maxine Burak

Art Director:
Sandra Ploy

Graphic Art Associates:
Ellen Lloyd, Catherine Fletcher,
Sarah Briggs

Chairman and Founder:
Roy Reiman

President:
Russell Denson

©2003 Reiman Media Group, Inc.
5400 S. 60th Street
Greendale, WI 53129

Country Books
International Standard Book Number 0-89821-382-7
Library of Congress Control Number 2003093735

For additional copies of this book or information
on other books, write: Country Books,
P.O. Box 990, Greendale, WI 53129.
Credit card orders call toll-free: 1-800/558-1013
or visit our Web site at **www.reimanpub.com**.

CHILDREN often say the funniest things, and for years *Country* and *Country EXTRA* readers have been sharing clever quips from the mouths of children for our long-running feature, "Little Humor".

Because that feature is so popular, we decided to publish this hardcover volume containing more than 500 of the "Little Humor" stories sent to us by parents, grandparents and others.

So, why not settle back in a comfy chair and get ready to share a chuckle or two? Thanks to our readers, we're sure you'll find more than a few!

LITTLE SPROUT. "Dylon was in our wheat field checking to see if the grain was ripe," says Leslie Niswonger of Wallace, Kansas.

Chuckles From Cherubs

God's gotta be smiling over these gems.

I WAS reading a Bible story about prophets to our friend's 5-year-old daughter, Kayleigh.

She asked me what a prophet was, and I told her it was someone who carried God's message to others.

She looked puzzled for a second, then remarked, "You know, I had a lemonade stand once and I drank up all my profits!"
— *Sue Haylor*
Kihei, Hawaii

 A LONG-WINDED visiting minister was still preaching at the time that our service normally ends. My young niece Kimberly leaned over and whispered, "Does he know what time we get out of here?"
— *Cora Detweiler*
Phoenix, Arizona

DANNY, our 2-year-old son, was always on the go. Sitting through a sermon on top of an hour of Sunday school was almost too much for him.

One Sunday, he was extra wiggly. I told him he'd have to wait until Daddy, who was the minister, said "Amen". Then he could go.

As my husband finished the prayer with "Amen", Danny shouted, "Amen! Let's go!"

He brought the house down.
— *Carol Watson*
Clyde, Ohio

MY FATHER died when my oldest daughter was only 2 years old. About a year later, she asked, "Mom, how did Grandpa get to Heaven? Did he drive?"

With a chuckle, I explained, "No, he didn't drive. Jesus came down and took Grandpa to Heaven with Him."

To this my daughter replied, "Oh, so Jesus drove."
— *Penny Nunn*
Croswell, Michigan

WHEN my mother died, our two youngest grandsons were told that Grandma had gone to Heaven. When their mother took them to the funeral home, 5-year-old Tony looked around in awe. Finally he said, "So, *this* is Heaven!"
— *Jerry Jackson*
Enid, Oklahoma

AFTER returning from a trip to the Holy Land, I gave my 5-year-old granddaughter a stone like the one David had used to slay the giant.

She took it to Sunday school, and when her teacher asked her where she got it, she said, "My grandma brought it from Heaven."
—*Betty Oates*
Harrisburg, Pennsylvania

MY GRANDSON Andrew had to sing in church and sit with his class up front. The minister was talking about missionaries and where they teach.

He then asked the children where they would like to go to teach. Andrew raised his hand, and when called upon, he proudly answered, "Disneyland!"
—*Charlotte Legate*
West Bend, Wisconsin

I WAS chaperoning a Girl Scout troop on a flight to Juneau, Alaska and sat right next to a 9-year-old

FACE IT! "My grandson Joe thinks the cold well water tastes good," says Betty Swanson of Silverton, Oregon.

who'd never flown before. After gazing out the window at the clouds awhile, she asked, "Are we in Heaven now?"
—*Mary Daubersmith*
Ward Cove, Alaska

MY GRANDDAUGHTER and her husband took their 3-year-old daughter, Kaylee, to church to see her baby cousin christened.

When they returned

What do you get if you cross a donkey with Christmas? Muletide greetings.

home, my daughter asked Kaylee if she saw baby Ashton. Kaylee replied, "Yes, and she got appetized in the birdbath!"

—*Ruth Davison*
Bloomington, Illinois

ON A fall day with my 8-year-old grandson, Richard, we noticed a cloud that resembled one of his favorite cartoon characters.

He turned to me and said, "Grandma, do you know what clouds are? They are God's Play-Doh."

—*Pamela Kramerage*
Martinsburg, West Virginia

MY granddaughter, Kyrsten, who was not yet 2, loved to sit with her daddy while he played the piano. At the end of each song, both of them raised their hands and yelled, "Done!"

Kyrsten's father filled in for the church pianist one Sunday. As the last chords of his closing medley drifted over the attentive congregation, a little voice yelled out from one of the pews, "Done!"

—*James McGarrity*
Doylestown, Ohio

WHEN our daughter, Lori, was born, she had a little 3-year-old cousin living nearby. Her name was Lisa.

Lisa had trouble remembering Lori's name. When she visited our house, she would often ask, "What is your baby's name?"

One day when I told her, Lisa's face suddenly lit up. "Oh, I remember!" she said. "Lori, Lori, hallelujah!"

—*Relda Leonard*
Columbia, South Carolina

WHEN my 4-year-old godson, John, was told that his godmother was coming to his house for dinner, he asked his mother, "Will she bring her wand?"

—*Miriam Trudeau*
Cheboygan, Michigan

MY 4-year-old niece, Brenda, was helping me do the

What do you get if you cross a suitcase with a pecan? A nut case.

GOT THE GIGGLES. "We were irrigating our yard when our grandkids Tyler and Shelby decided to play in the water," says Nancy Woods from Safford, Arizona. "It looks like they had lots of fun splashing around!"

dishes. She looked out the window and saw a jet streak forming high in the sky, with the back end of it widening and fading.

"Look, Aunt Joanne," she said, "look where God is drawing!" —*Joanne Mayur*
Attica, New York

MY husband and I took our 6-year-old grandson, David, hiking with us one day on his "day off" from kindergarten.

On our way to the woods, my husband, Phil, was commenting with frustration on the cloudy, cool day, since the forecast had called for warm, sunny weather.

David observed, "Maybe Jesus couldn't make a decision." —*Kathy Lutz*
Cook, Minnesota

ONE NIGHT while getting my two boys ready for bed, I told them I would read a new Bible story.

The older one said, "You mean there are more stories in the Bible?"

The younger one answered, "Oh, yes, those people in Heaven are always doing something new."
—*Lois Shenold*
Littleton, Colorado

I HAD fixed lunch for my grandson Charles, 2, and asked him if he would like to thank God for his food.

He folded his little hands and said, "Dear God, thank you for this food. Take care of all the good people...and do what you want with the bad ones."
—*Ruth Ann Bodenhausen*
St. Joseph, Missouri

RIDING HOME from Sunday school, I asked my 3-year-old son what he'd studied that day. "We learned all about Noah's ark and how the fudge covered the Earth!" he replied.
—*Julie Popenfoose*
Tacoma, Washington

MY NEPHEW Lucas, 3, was visiting our Sunday school, where they were teaching the children songs for our approaching Christmas program.

Driving home later, his mother asked what songs he learned. "Well," said Lucas, "we learned one about a bad dog that had fleas."

Drawing a complete blank on that song, his mother asked him to sing a little of it. So Lucas started singing, "Fleas, naughty dog..."

That's all it took for his mother to recognize the song as the Spanish Christmas carol, *Feliz Navidad.*
—*Jodi Bock*
Foxholm, North Dakota

ONE SUNDAY, my 7-year-old niece, Courtney, attended church with us.

Before the service, my husband and I pointed out the people who appeared in the stained-glass windows. Then I pointed out Jesus on the cross.

Courtney stared quietly for a moment, then turned to me and said, "You know, he looks a lot like his father." —*Candyce Pospisil*
Baltimore, Maryland

I HAD just returned home with a craft project I was working on, and our 4-year-old grandson asked me why I was making it. I explained that it kept my hands busy, as idle hands were the devil's workshop.

A few weeks later, he saw the finished product

and said, "Grandma, did you make that at the devil's workshop?"

—*Betty Hemminger*
Riverside, California

ONE afternoon a friend stopped by to visit with my three boys and found my youngest son, Kevin, "sputtering" to himself.

She asked what was wrong, and Kevin replied, "Germs and Jesus, germs and Jesus—that's all I ever hear, and I've never seen either one of them!"

—*Nola Owen*
Virginia Beach, Virginia

WHEN 4-year-old David was saying his evening prayers, he was told to ask for a safe trip for his grandfather, who was traveling to Texas.

"Mama," David asked, "what kind of car will I tell God that Grandpa is driving?"   —*V. Susan Barth*
Green Bay, Wisconsin

AT THE CLOSE of a church service, our pastor asked, "Does anyone have anything they'd like to say?"

Our youngest son, not quite old enough for kindergarten, spoke up,

DOING A DOUBLE TAKE. "We took our country granddaughter Emily to the department store and she was fascinated with what she saw—herself!" explains Glenda Adams of Winter Haven, Florida. "I'm glad I had my camera handy."

"I'm sleepy and I want to go home!"   —*Ruby Brewer Waynesboro, Mississippi*

ROSS loves the outdoors, but since he was to start kindergarten soon, his mother tried to get him interested in coloring. She stressed how important it was to "stay in the lines".

One evening a few days later, Ross and his mother were riding home in the car when she pointed to the sunset and remarked, "Isn't that pretty?"

Ross looked up and added, "It sure is. God sure stays in the lines good, doesn't He?"

—*Mrs. Henry Boluis Parkersburg, Iowa*

WHILE VISITING my son and his family, we attended church with them.

When it came time for the ushers to gather the offering, our grandson, Eric, 5, asked his mom for her contribution so he could put it in the collection plate.

As an usher approached, I reached for my wallet. When Eric saw this, he said loudly, "Grandpa, put your

PERFECTLY SIT-UATED. "Son Wade hams it up for the camera," says Rose Ann Lemieux, Menominee, Mich.

money away. I'll pay the bill."   —*Joe Suminski Centerville, Indiana*

WE TOOK our grandson Michael, 5, to church with us. During Communion, when the usher came by with the bread and grape juice, Michael said, "No thanks. I'm having lunch at Grandma's today."

—*Norma Stowers Heath, Ohio*

ONE NIGHT our two boys, ages 4 and 5, were saying their prayers. Based on what we heard, the 4-year-old had evidently had a difficult day on the farm.

The 5-year-old ended his prayer with: "And God bless everything that walks on two feet."

And the 4-year-old added, "Except the chickens."

—*Florence Backman*
Clarence, Iowa

WHILE VISITING her grandma one day, our daughter Samantha looked up and saw a skywriter at work. With an amazed look on her face, she asked, "Is God writing that?"

—*Kim Carlton*
Arcadia, California

OUR SON and his family joined us for Sunday worship services. As 10 men went to the front to begin the Communion service and the preacher said a prayer, Borden, our 3-year-old grandson, asked who the man was and what was he doing.

Our son told Borden that the man was the preacher,
and he was talking to God.

Borden scrutinized each of the other 10 men and asked, "Which one is God?"

—*Helen Fleetwood*
Alton, Illinois

I WAS sitting on the porch swing talking with my 4-year-old granddaughter, Courtney, when she said, "You know, Nana, God made me."

Then Courtney sighed and added, "God made you, too, Nana. But he made you out of a lot of parts that hurt." —*Betty Smith*
Newry, Pennsylvania

AFTER attending church services with us on the Fourth of July, our 3-year-old grandson told his mother, "In church we sang 'Oh Beautiful for Spaceship Skies'!" —*Delores Ewing*
Glenwood, Minnesota

I WENT into the kitchen just in time to see my granddaughter stick her

---

What works only after it's been fired?
A rocket.

hand in the cookie jar.

When she saw me, she quickly pulled her hand out, replaced the lid and said, "The devil isn't getting far with me these days, is he?"

—*Mrs. Leonard Workman*
Wichita, Kansas

DURING Sunday school class, I noticed that one of the 4-year-olds was coloring a picture of a lamb bright green and had drawn what appeared to be three large buttons on its side.

When I inquired about her unusual lamb, she explained, "This way, if they make a sweater out of him, he'll already be colored and have buttons!"

—*Sharon Johnson*
Soddy Daisy, Tennessee

WHEN our oldest daughter, Beth, was very small, her bedtime prayer was, "Dear Jesus, watch over us tonight."

But it didn't come out quite the same when she said, "Dear Jesus, please watch out and don't run over us tonight!"

—*Mary Brown*
Richton, Mississippi

FOR YEARS as a child, I was under the impression I had to eat peas to get to Heaven. That's because, every Christmas, my family gathered around the old piano to sing *Silent Night*...and I thought the words went: "Sleep in Heaven, eat peas."

It wasn't until I was older that I found out the line was "Sleep in heavenly peace".—*Sylvia Sinneborn*
York, Pennsylvania

MY 2-year-old granddaughter, Katie, loves to play hide-and-seek.

When she was in church with her parents, the priest bowed behind the altar.

Katie, who was watching intently, asked in a *loud* voice, "Is Father Joe hiding?"
—*Pat Luther*
Milwaukee, Wisconsin

What time is it when an elephant sits on a fence? Time to fix the fence.

WHEN OUR son Ronny was little, we never gave him money because he put everything in his mouth.

One Sunday, as we were about to leave for church, he ran to a closet and began looking intently for something. We waited patiently, wondering what he was doing.

A few minutes later, he came running to us with a big smile on his face—and a handful of Monopoly money. From then on, we gave him real money for the church collection.

—*Ron and Peggy Bauer*
Augusta, Kansas

WHEN OUR daughter was 4, she often forgot to close the door when coming in from outside. Finally, I scolded her, "Shut the door. Were you born in a barn?"

She looked at me and responded softly, "No, but Jesus was." —*Thom Borchert*
Bella Vista, Arkansas

WE WERE driving home from church with our 5-year-old grandson, Reed, when he asked whether God was everywhere. We assured him that God was indeed everywhere.

Then he asked whether God was in the car...and again, we assured him that He was.

At that, Reed looked into the backseat and said, "God, do you have your seatbelt on?"

—*June Dempsey*
Boulder, Colorado

DURING the morning worship service at our church, we have a "time for children" segment. On this particular day, the lady in

MUDDY MONSTER. "Grant decided playing in the mud was fun," says his mom, Tracy Johnson, Bethany, Conn.

charge was explaining how Christians are the "light, salt and leaven" of the world.

The children understood light and salt, but when she asked them what leaven was, they were silent. Then my 6-year-old grandson spoke up.

"It's what comes after 10!" Kevin replied.
—*Viola Lundry*
Oelwein, Iowa

MY YOUNG grandson Spencer told me he was playing ball with God. "How do you do that?" I asked.

He replied, "Well, I throw the ball up to God, and He throws it back to me."
—*Lanelle Bozeman*
Lumberton, Texas

A CHILD was talking in church, so her mother hushed her and said, "You must be quiet because this is God's house."

"Where is God?" the little girl asked.

"He's in Heaven."

"Well," the little girl said. "He'd better come home pretty quick, because He's got lots of company."
—*Karen Ann Bland*
Gove, Kansas

I ASKED my 4-year-old grandson who made him.

"God," Eric replied.

"Do you know why?" I asked.

"I guess he just got tired of dinosaurs," he answered.
—*Josephine Werenski*
North Chicago, Illinois

MY husband, who is a minister, announced in church one Sunday that there would be a wedding shower for one of the young ladies of the congregation.

Our 4-year-old daughter, Lisa, wanted to know if she could go along, and I told her that she could.

That's when she asked, "Do we have to bring our own towels?"—*Patty Harper*
Henderson, North Carolina

OUR 3-year-old nephew, Garren, was fascinated with cameras and photography. One night a bright flash of lightning lit up the whole sky. Garren turned

SPLASHDOWN. "One day Devin discovered it's just too hard to resist playing in a spring puddle," says his Grandma Carol from Killbuck, Ohio.

to his mom and said, "God must be taking pictures."
—*Sherry McCarver*
Marietta, Georgia

BREANN, our 4-year-old granddaughter, was lying contentedly on my lap one Sunday morning and gazing up at the ceiling. She looked at me and asked, "If our prayers go up to God, who fixes all the holes in the ceiling?"—*Fern Bigham*
Lubbock, Texas

WHEN OUR son was young, my husband and I would allow him to crawl in bed with us on weekends. The bed was positioned in front of a window that faced east.

One Saturday he stood looking out the window for the longest time and gave a great sigh as the sun appeared over the horizon.

"Well," our son said, "He finally turned the light on."
—*Ruth Hunter*
Brisbane, California

OUR 3-year-old daughter, Hannah, had a crush on a 10-year-old boy, Jonathan, from our church. After the

"Please tell me, because I would like to know, too," I answered.

"That's easy," he replied. "It's when the angels are taking their showers."
—*Ruth Hunter*
Brisbane, California

BEFORE the service for my son Brandon's First Communion, our priest announced to the congregation that he was going to keep his homily short. He explained that Brandon had spoken to him before church and said, "Speed things up. I have a party to go to." —*Debbie Ryan*
DeWitt, Michigan

PIT STOP. "Our daughter Sydney enjoys peaches from our orchard," says Gretchen Glick of Thompson, Pa.

service one Sunday, Hannah told us that she loved Jonathan.

My husband quickly said, "Hannah, you're only 3 years old. You don't even know what love is yet."

Hannah looked up at her dad with the most serious expression on her face and answered, "Yes, I do. I love you, Daddy."
—*Sharon Graham*
Cleveland, Tennessee

MY NEPHEW is a very smart child. "I know what makes it rain," he said.

OUR CHURCH sponsored a community picnic and invited families of all religions to attend. Our daughter Kimberly, then 7, was having a great time, making new friends with playmates from different denominations.

Kim wanted to express her appreciation, so she skipped over to our minister, tugged on his coat and bubbled, "This is the best picnic ever, Reverend! There must be kids here from every abomination in the world!"

Fortunately, our minister noticed the wide-open spaces awaiting Kim's two front teeth, and he thanked her for the compliment!

—*Diane Falkner*
Madison, Wisconsin

"MOMMY, I've got a stomachache," said Nellie, the 6-year-old daughter of a friend.

"That's because your stomach is empty," her mother replied. "As soon as you eat something, you'll feel better."

That afternoon, the pastor stopped by for a visit. He happened to mention that he had a headache.

Nellie piped up, "You'd feel better if you had something in it."

—*Villard Brida*
Springfield, Missouri

MY NEPHEW Aaron is quite a picky eater. One evening, his mom insisted he eat the casserole she prepared.

But before she dished up the food, it was Aaron's turn to say grace, and he began, "Dear God, please don't make me eat this."

—*Amy Drabek*
Moore, Oklahoma

WHEN my son Greg was about 4, we went for a long drive one fall day. As we drove along, I commented on how bare the trees looked.

After a moment of thought, Greg said, "Maybe God should've glued the leaves on better."

—*Vonnie Entzminger*
Jamestown, North Dakota

THE TEACHER at Sunday school asked my 8-year-old niece, Julianne, to define the word "humility". She thought for a moment and replied, "It's when you're real smart like I am, but you don't go around telling everybody."

—*Brenda Walker*
Imperial, Missouri

WHILE DRESSING my kids for outside play, I couldn't find my 3-year-old daughter's boots.

I asked where she'd left

them only to be informed that they were buried outside!

With shovel in hand, I marched outside to dig in the area she pointed to. After two attempts—one sock...then another...then the boots.

My question about boot burial was answered back inside when 5-year-old Gavin explained, "Well, Jayna, they didn't go to Heaven!" —*Beth Bastian Snohomish, Washington*

HAY THERE! "Tony and Maggie like playing in haystacks," says Grandma Melva Avila, San Luis Obispo, Calif.

MY 4-year-old son, Tanner, and my father were drawing on the sidewalk with chalk. While Dad was busy, Tanner had managed to draw all over our steps.

Dad asked Tanner what he thought I would do when I saw this. Knowing it took water to wash off the chalk, Tanner said, "Grandpa, I think we better start praying for rain."

—*Jana Mayo Gallant, Alabama*

WHILE SITTING on the porch swing one evening with our 2-year-old grandson, Isaac, he noticed the beautiful sunset. He turned to me and asked, "Grandma, who made that?"

I replied, "Jesus did."

A couple of weeks later, we were walking outside after a rainstorm. Threatening clouds still filled the skies. Isaac looked at them and said, "Grandma, Jesus sure made a mess, didn't he?" —*Joyce Carroll Salem, Indiana*

THERE'S 10 months' difference between our daughter Meredith, who is 5, and her curly headed playmate Katelyn. One evening after pondering this age difference,

Meredith said, "I know why I was born before Katelyn. It took Jesus a long time to make all of her curls."
—*Carol Addis*
Shelby, North Carolina

AT CHURCH, our 4-year-old grandson, Jonathan, was asked to offer some "good intentions" along with the other children.

When it was his turn, he said, "I'd like God to take care of all the grandmas and grandpas and all the old people living in restrooms."   —*Jan Thompson*
Jackson, Tennessee

I DIDN'T REALIZE how much today's children have become dependent on automobiles until my 4-year-old son asked, "When you go to Heaven, who drives the car back?"   —*Laurie Jacobs*
Grafton, Wisconsin

THE CHILDREN of our congregation are invited to the front of church every Sunday for a brief sermon especially for them.

One Sunday the topic was birthdays, and the leader asked, "Why do we have birthdays?"

Tessa Moxley, a 3-year-old in the group, replied, "Because we can't get bigger if we don't have birthdays."   —*Walter Collins*
Mountain Rest,
South Carolina

DURING a drive through the Texas Hill Country, my son commented to his son, "Why don't we take these beautiful hills and river home with us?"

"We can't do that, Daddy," my grandson replied. "God glued them here."
—*Jessima Tumlinson*
Ingram, Texas

MY daughter and her children came to visit, and the kids were especially excited because they planned to fly kites in the wide-open spaces.

However, their mother

What do cows like to dance to?
Any kind of moosic.

remarked that it might not be possible because it was *too* windy.

Scott, who was 4 at the time, supplied the explanation for that: "Yes, Grandma. Jesus just turned on his fan." —*Pearl Whisenand Higbee, Missouri*

WHEN my sons Trey and Michael were 3 and 4 years old, the first Bible verse I taught them was, "Be ye kind, one to the other".

A few days later, the boys' little friend Wes came to play with them, and I noticed Michael running into our den.

In a flash, Michael was back with my Bible. I smiled, thinking it was so sweet that he was going to share the Bible verse with Wes.

The next thing I heard was Wes yelling for help. Apparently he had taken one of Trey's toys, and there was Michael hitting Wes with the Bible. All the while, Michael was exclaiming, "The Bible says be ye kind to one anudder, Wes!" —*GeNeil Avery Tuscaloosa, Alabama*

ONE Sunday morning, I heard my little 8-year-old cousins, Lauren and Heidi, talking in the restroom at church.

"Last week I pulled my tooth here and dropped it," Lauren said. "Luckily I found it, though."

"I bet you're glad," Heidi replied. "The tooth fairy might have donated your money to the church." —*Celesa Willett Waynesville, North Carolina*

OUR sons Wade and Stacy shared a room when they were young. Wade went to bed early one night because he was tired.

A little later, Stacy also headed to bed. I stepped in to say good night to him and asked if he had said his prayers for the night.

"No, I can't, because Wade is sleeping," Stacy

Why is it smart to buy a bird for a pet? Because they're cheep.

answered innocently.

"You don't have to say them aloud," I explained. "You can just think them."

Stacy gave me a startled look and said, "I didn't know that God could read minds." —*Donna Taylor Orrtanna, Pennsylvania*

OUR children frowned when I put the roast beef and rice on the table, but they knew better than to say "yuck". Dutifully, each said a prayer.

McKenna said, "Thank you, God, for roast beef and rice."

Connor was somewhat more honest. "Thank you, God, for roast beef," he said.

Reece closed his eyes and prayed, "Thank you, God, for pancakes."
—*Tammy Barley Folsom, California*

HAND IN HAND. "Our young friends Jansen and Madeline looked so cute while taking a stroll in Rocky Mountain National Park," says Tara Guenzi from Sterling, Ohio.

WHO ME? "Great-nephew Kaleb Bausch got caught white-handed in the flour bin," says Ruth Nelson, Silver Star, Montana.

From the Mouths Of Little Sprouts

Table talk that's food
for the funny bone.

GETTING AN EARFUL. Young McKenzie "rows" along a delicious cob of corn. Parents Steve and Sheryl Wright from Lachine, Michigan submitted the photo.

OUR 4-year-old grandson, Michael, was staying the night with us. When he woke up, my wife asked him what he wanted to eat for breakfast.

"What can you make, Grandma, that I can put ketchup on?" was his reply.
—*Al Mormann*
Costa Mesa, California

WHILE fixing hamburgers for her family's dinner, my daughter-in-law roasted and peeled some green chilies, which she placed on the plate of "fixin's".

When Sheila, her 4-year-old, came to the table and saw the long green chilies, she said to her brother, "Look! A dead pickle."
—*Sue Hood*
Harley, New Mexico

AS I ATE breakfast one day with my great-grandson Evan, I noticed him dubiously holding a hard-boiled egg in the shell.

He turned to me and asked, "Great-Grandma, will you please hatch this egg for me?" —*Eva Kobes*
Zeeland, Michigan

COMING into the kitchen one day, I found our lively

2-year-old had climbed up on the counter and retrieved a box of cookies from the cupboard. He gave a quick look at the printing on the box and explained, "I was just reading the directions."

"And what do the directions say?" I asked.

He answered without hesitation, "They say, 'You can have some.'"

—*Don Williams*
Raynham, Massachusetts

MY AUNT'S grandson came to visit her and announced when he walked in the door, "Grandma, I came for hugs and kisses, biscuits and gravy."

—*Thelma McKiddy*
Pacific Junction, Iowa

A FRIEND who was taking care of my daughters one day introduced them to some foods they hadn't eaten at home—like tuna.

Not long afterward, I asked my girls what they wanted for lunch. My 4-

year-old piped up, "I want a, you know, petunia fish sandwich." —*Linda Miller*
Gardiner, Montana

WHEN I asked my 6-year-old granddaughter how she liked the turkey dinner I had fixed, she replied, "I didn't like the turkey, but I really liked the bread he ate."

—*Lucille Duncan*
Willis, Virginia

OUR FAMILY spent a week camping in the High Sierras on horseback. After being jumbled and jerked to pieces for 5 long hours, I said to my 9-year-old daughter, "I feel like a milk shake."

She, obviously hungry, replied, "I feel like a hamburger and fries."

—*Janice Jones*
Lemoore, California

MY DAUGHTER Jamie, 3, was sitting down with me to taste her first piece of zucchini bread. She stared at it

What should you put in a barrel of water to make it lighter? A hole.

awhile, then took a bite.

When I asked her if she liked it, she replied, "It's good, but there's a little bit of grass in it, Mom!"

—*Tammy Bender*
Midland, Pennsylvania

MY 3-year-old grandson, Cody, was spending the day with me. At lunchtime, I gave him some gelatin with pineapple in it.

When his dad came to take him home, Cody said, "Dad, Grandma puts pine needles in her Jell-O."

—*Cora Kime*
Aspers, Pennsylvania

WE received a rare snowfall one Friday evening. Since my husband had to work Saturday morning and knew he wouldn't be able to play in the snow with our daughter Julie, he made two snowballs and put them in the freezer.

When she woke up, Julie was thrilled to learn of the surprise her dad had left her. But after picking one up and holding it a minute, her hands got cold.

So she handed it to me, pointed to the microwave and asked, "Mommy, can you warm this up for me?"

—*Denise Peters*
Loveland, Ohio

MY SISTER Nola made an apple pie with a double crust and put it in the oven, which had a small window on the door.

As the pie baked and bubbled, the crust began to rise and fall with the heat.

My 4-year-old niece, Vicky, watched in amazement and said, "Look, Mommy, look! The pie is breathing!" —*Wendy Alvarez*
Broken Arrow, Oklahoma

SWEET REWARD. "Grandson Garrett likes to lick the spatula when we bake," says Darlean Goskey, Rogers, Minn.

ONE DAY as I was getting a gallon of milk out of the refrigerator, I dropped it.

Fortunately, the bottle did not break, but the lid came off, sending milk everywhere.

My 9-year-old son exclaimed, "Boy, Mom, I didn't think a gallon of milk could go that far!"

—Lissa Landru
Aitkin, Minnesota

IT WAS Thanksgiving and our 2-year-old granddaughter, Jocelyn, had arrived with her parents for dinner. As soon as she walked in the door, she wanted to see the desserts, so I showed her the boysenberry, chocolate and lemon pies.

After dinner, Jocelyn announced, "I want a piece of that boys and girls pie."

—Mayme Kulper
Gonzales, California

OUR grandson Chad, 3, is very fond of meatballs. He came by one afternoon as we were finishing a meal of meatballs and gravy.

He looked the table over, and then said in a very serious voice, "Grandma, that meatball really wants me!"

—Goldie Fields
Upton, Kentucky

OUR 9-year-old son often prepares food in our microwave when he comes home from school.

One day our microwave was broken, so I explained how he'd have to put the food in a pan, put it on the stove, turn on the burner and stir the food.

When his food was done, he asked me, "Gee, Mom, where did you learn that neat trick?"

—Jean Christenson
Lester Prairie, Minnesota

I TEACH at a university child development center. My plan for the morning was to discuss restaurants and then have the children play the roles of hostess, waiter, cashier, etc.

I asked the children where they would go to eat if their mom or dad didn't feel like cooking, trying to get them to say "restaurant".

That's when Sara's eyes lit up and a big smile crossed her face. She excitedly answered, "Grandma's house." —*Linda Carson Emporia, Kansas*

SHORTLY after our daughter Kaitlin, 4, became aware that her grandmother had false teeth, we took the family to a restaurant.

Kaitlin must've thought the food was delicious, because she yelled over the noise of the crowd, "Grandma, aren't you glad you brought your teeth?"

—*Brenda Jandereski Port Austin, Michigan*

MY granddaughter Katie was helping me bake a special cake. She read the instructions as we proceeded. When the batter didn't look quite right, I read over the recipe myself and noticed it called for three egg *whites*. We had put in three eggs.

After I told her about the error, she replied, "But, Grandma, I picked the three whitest eggs I could find." —*Marcine Bailey Beach Park, Illinois*

AT DINNER, my husband told our 3-year-old granddaughter, Alexis, "Clean your plate, and you'll get bigger."

"No, I'll get dessert," Alexis replied.

—*Marjorie Bushey Middlebury, Vermont*

WHILE I was baking one afternoon, my 4-year-old son asked what kind of cake I was making. "A marble cake," I replied.

As I served the cake after dinner that evening, my husband commented on how delicious it was.

"Not really, Daddy," said our son. "She forgot the marbles." —*Ardelle Hill Santa Barbara, California*

I RAN OUT of milk during a visit from my two little grandsons. So I mixed up a jug of powdered milk to get by for the rest of the day.

When I took my grandsons home that evening, they excitedly told their mother, "Mom, guess what

---

What's as big as an elephant but weighs nothing? His shadow.

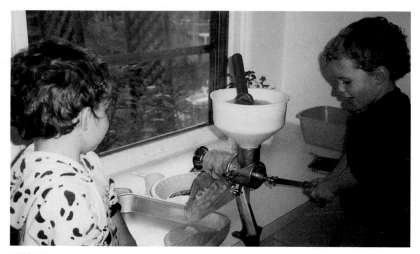

KITCHEN CREW. "My twin grandsons, John and Matthew, are the best helpers around, especially when it comes to making applesauce," says Darlene Kelley, Apopka, Fla.

Grandma did. She made homemade milk!"

—*Dorothy Cayton*
Lost Creek, West Virginia

MY FAMILY went to eat at a buffet-style restaurant. After we had gone through the serving line, our waitress asked if everything was okay.

"Everything but the peanut butter," answered our son, Artie, 8.

We didn't know what he was talking about, until we realized he had taken liver pate, thinking it was peanut butter!

—*Loretta Latta*
Gilboa, New York

AS I BROWSED through cookbooks one day in search of that perfect fudge recipe, I remarked that I didn't have a candy thermometer.

Son Ben, who was 5, overheard me and commented, "Mom, I didn't know candy got sick!"

—*Barbara Gebauer*
Amelia, Ohio

WE TOOK our 7-year-old son, Hunter, to a country restaurant one evening. As the hostess seated us, she informed us that they were fresh out of corn bread muffins.

When the waitress came

to take our order, she told us there were no more baked potatoes.

A short time later, the power went out in the restaurant. As we sat in total darkness, Hunter piped up, "Mom, are they out of electricity, too?"

—Timothy McCracken
Cleveland, Tennessee

I BURNED some biscuits one morning, so I offered our son, Elijah, a very ripe banana instead. After eyeing the black spots on it, Elijah said sympathetically, "Mom, I think you burned the banana, too."

—Victoria Bell
Spencer, Wisconsin

WHILE growing up, my younger sister, Robin, always seemed to be hungry.

When Robin was about 5, our mom prepared lunch for us. After we had finished, Robin said she was hungry. Mom gave her an apple. Robin ate it and said she was still hungry.

Mom gave her a slice of toast, but Robin said she still wanted more to eat. Mom told her she could have a few cookies, which Robin gobbled down.

Again, Robin said she was hungry. Exasperated, Mom said, "Robin, there is a limit!"

Robin replied, "Okay, I'll have one of those, too."

—Toni Heisey
Susanville, California

ONE DAY while baking, our 3-year-old daughter, Hannah, asked me, "Why do we have two stoves?"

"The stove in the basement burns wood to keep us warm in the winter," I explained.

"Oh," she replied. "Then this one in the kitchen burns food."

—Bethany Keeney
Seven Valleys, Pennsylvania

I MADE popcorn one evening and gave a bowl to our daughter Marleigh, who was 2. Then I added caramel to the rest to make caramel popcorn for myself.

Marleigh saw this and wanted a taste, so she ran to get her bowl. "I want gravy, too," she said.

—Camille Biorn
Pocatello, Idaho

OUR 5-year-old grandson, Mitch, was getting tired and cranky waiting for dessert to be served. "I think it's time for B-E-D," I said to him. "Do you know what that spells?"

"Pie!" he replied hopefully. —*Betty Gering* *Issaquah, Washington*

I'D PREPARED a hearty breakfast of biscuits and gravy, sausage, eggs and hash browns. Our 4-year-old daughter, Stephanie, ate more than usual.

Afterward, while I was sitting on the couch, Stephanie crawled up on my lap. She laughed and

STEP RIGHT UP! Hannah Bowman can stand tall when it comes to helping in the kitchen, says Grandma Elizabeth Lindquist from Bemus Point, New York.

said, "Feel my tummy."

"Do you have a stomachache?" I asked.

"No," she replied. "Feel it. My tummy's just grinning."
—*Marie Parker, Edna, Texas*

OUR CHURCH was having a large potluck dinner in honor of a member's 90th birthday. After surveying all the food on the table, 7-year-old Jordan Scott said, "I can't believe they don't have one peanut butter and jelly sandwich."
—*Dollye Harberger*
Ironton, Ohio

MY NIECE'S 4-year-old boy, Christopher, loves Mexican food. At a restaurant he was eating taco chips, dipping them in hot salsa.

After a few of them, he laid one chip down on his napkin and said, "I think I'll let it cool awhile."
—*Emma Bartholomew*
Riverside, California

MY NEPHEW Johnny, 6, was a fussy eater. To encourage him to clean his plate, his mother explained

BIRTHDAY BOY. "Zachary devoured his first birthday cake," says Grandpa Robert Robinson, Yorba Linda, Calif.

that in poor countries, people had to eat the peels from potatoes.

Johnny thought about that for a moment and asked, "Well, what do they do with the potatoes?"
—*Irene Maki*
Chatham, Michigan

ONE AFTERNOON I was baby-sitting at an area health club. One of the little boys decided to have his lunch.

He dug in and, in short order, he had polished off everything completely except for an apple.

After three or four bites, he put it down and said, "I can't finish this. I think I have lost my 'apple-tite'."
—*Kelly Kapper*
Decatur, Illinois

I WAS discussing the importance of milk with our 4-year-old grandson, Andrew. The conversation led us to list a variety of foods made from milk, including ice cream, cheese and yogurt.

"And butter," I added.

"Oh, no," Andrew corrected me. "We get butter from butterflies!"   —*Carol Hughes*
Port Charlotte, Florida

I REMEMBER the time my younger brother's chin quivered and tears started to flow when he was offered some au gratin potatoes.

"I don't want any old rotten potatoes," he said.

Our family has used that term for au gratin potatoes ever since!

—*Nadine Prevetti*
Milwaukee, Wisconsin

MY NIECE doesn't like potatoes, but she *loves* french fries.

One day, Grandma took her out for lunch at a restaurant. She was eating french fries when she came upon one that was broken in half.

"Oh, yuck, Grandma," she said. "You eat this one—it has potato in it!"

—*Karen Johnson*
Naknek, Alaska

OUR SON Ken was watching closely as his dad mixed some cake batter.

When my husband added the eggs, he cracked them open on the edge of the counter. Ken looked puzzled, then finally said, "But, Daddy! Mommy always hatches her eggs on the bowl."   —*Joan Lulow*
Salem, Oregon

I WAS showing our son Tyler, 4, a bicentennial silver dollar.

I pointed out the bell on the back of the coin and asked him if he knew what it was called.

"Sure I know!" he replied. "It's the Taco Bell!"

—*Jacque Hayden*
Bardwell, Kentucky

How can you feed 10 people with only eight potatoes? Mash 'em.

FISHING BUDDIES. "My dad, Charlie, and nephew Joseph both enjoy fishing," says Ginger Peacock of Haysville, Kansas.

Grand Kicks From Grandkids

There's no telling what grandchildren will say to Grandma and Grandpa.

OUR SON and daughter-in-law had a new baby. When the minister visited to discuss plans for the baby's baptism, he immediately struck up a conversation with 4-year-old Megan.

In the course of the conversation, Megan stated in an all-knowing way that boys and girls are different.

While the minister hesitated as to what to say next, she hurried on to explain, "Little girls have Mickey Mouse on their underpants and little boys have robots on theirs!"

—*Bernell Baldwin*
Newton, Kansas

CASTING AWAY. "Jake likes to fish off our dock with Grandpa Dick," says Kathleen Brown of Eudora, Kansas.

I WAS chewing bubble gum and offered a piece to my 3-year-old granddaughter, Carrie. She watched me blow a bubble and said, "Grandpa, will you put some air in mine, too?"

—*John Anderson*
State College, Pennsylvania

A FEW WEEKS after my granddaughter Ashlynd was born, I picked up her 7-year-old brother, Ryan. We were driving along when out of the blue, Ryan informed me, "Ashlynd lost her extension cord."

I was puzzled...then chuckled when I figured out Ryan was referring to his sister's umbilical cord.

—*Mary Joslin*
Mt. Pleasant, Michigan

MY WIFE was looking at a magazine with our little grandson Duke. She turned to a page that included a perfume sample.

She told Duke to tear out the ad and put it in his underwear drawer. "It'll make your underwear smell real nice," she said.

"But, Grandma," Duke replied, "who would want to smell my underwear?"

—Robert Killackey
Sun Lakes, Arizona

WHILE I was visiting my daughter, my little granddaughter lost a tooth. She put it under her pillow that night, and the tooth fairy left her a shiny quarter.

The next evening, my granddaughter asked me for my dentures. When I asked why, she said, "So the tooth fairy can leave me lots of money."

—Emma Stilling
Santa Barbara, California

I WAS baby-sitting my grandson Cory, 4, on a rainy day. He was tired of being cooped up inside, so I told him he could ride his toy tractor in the carport.

With each trip around the carport, Cory widened his circle until he was out in the rain. "Cory, get back in the carport before you're soaked," I told him. "You'll get a sore throat."

"I won't get a sore throat, Nana, 'cause I'm gonna keep my mouth closed," Cory replied.

—Kathy Warren
Philadelphia, Mississippi

I WAS driv-  ing over a series of hills with my 5-year-old granddaughter, Amy. It had been a long drive, so in an effort to entertain her, I said, "Chug, chug, chug and up the hill we go." As we reached the top, I said, "Whee, here we go down the hill."

After repeating this for the third hill we went over, Amy burst my bubble by saying, "Grandpa, you're acting just like a 2-year-old."   *—Wendell Robinette*
Lockeford, California

ONE DAY I went shopping with my two young grandsons, David, 4, and Steve, 1.

Dave wandered away, and when he realized he was lost, he went to the customer service desk and told them his name.

When they asked if he was lost, he said, "No, but my grandma is."

So over the loudspeaker

they announced, "We have a little boy by the name of David Stier who states that he's not lost but his grandma is. Will she please come and claim him?"

—*Mary Kinnee*
Marine City, Michigan

WE WERE having a birthday gathering for one of our grandsons, and I was in the kitchen preparing food when I glanced into our bedroom.

Stevie, 7, and his brother Chris, 4, were jumping on the bed. Since this is not allowed in our house, I immediately put a stop to it.

"Hey!" I said. "There's a whole outside to play in, so go play in it."

Chris jumped off the bed, looked at me quizzically and asked, "Grandma, where is that hole?"

—*Virginia Bunce*
Corry, Pennsylvania

ONE MORNING my 3-year-old granddaughter, Elisa, asked if she could brush my hair. Since I'm bald on the top of my head, she started brushing the hair above my ears.

Then she stopped, looked

CHATTING WITH GRANDPA. "While visiting one day, our granddaughter Danielle had a heart to heart with my husband, Harold," says Gladys DeBoer, Castleford, Ind.

up at me and very seriously said, "Granddad, I'll be gentle. I don't want to knock any more hair off."

—*Terence Davis*
Chadron, Nebraska

WHEN our grandson Brandon was 4, I asked him what he'd like to be when he grew up. He answered, "I want to be a knight."

I asked how he was going to do that. Brandon immediately replied, "I'm going to go to night school."

—*R.J. Sellers*
Kittanning, Pennsylvania

I WAS playing "store" with my 2-year-old granddaughter, Maggie, and it's sure not the same game of pretend it used to be. When I asked Maggie for a loaf of bread, she pointed over her shoulder and said, "It's in aisle one."

—*Marcelle Crean*
Southbury, Connecticut

MY 3-YEAR-OLD granddaughter's new baby sister had just come home from the hospital, so I called to see how things were going.

"I'm just fine," my granddaughter told me.

"And how's the baby?" I asked, though I could hear the little one crying in the background.

"Well," my granddaughter answered, "she's half fine."

—*Mildred Danenhirsch*
Bayville, New York

OUR grandson Joseph went fishing for the first time when he was 3. He really got a kick out of putting worms on his hook and was equally excited when he pulled out several large fish.

Finally, Joseph turned around and said, "What I don't understand is how those worms turn into fish!"

—*Jim and Claudia Hart*
Green Valley, Arizona

MY 3-year-old granddaughter and I were sitting on the porch swing shelling peas together. After several minutes, she looked up at me and said, "Grandmother, I need to wash my hands."

I replied, "We will be finished shelling in just a few minutes. Why not wait and wash them then?"

She looked me square in the eye and said, "Grandmother, I *need* to suck my thumb!"

—Annie Ruth Parrish
Deep Run, North Carolina

ONE HOT July day, my 5-year-old grandson, Evan, was observing the saliva dripping from our panting dog's mouth. Turning to me, he asked, "Grandma, is the dog melting?"

—Arlene Ruth Bush
Morrison, Illinois

MY great-granddaughter Anna, 3, was visiting me one day and said, "My daddy says you're my great-grandma instead of my grandma. What is it that makes you so great?"

—Helen Haggart
Mt. Pleasant, Michigan

FOUR-YEAR-OLD Jeremy is a dead ringer for his grandfather, in every way.

Riding with Jeremy in his truck and plagued by the boy's constant "whys", Grandpa finally asked him, "Why do you ask so many questions?"

The little guy thought for a few moments, then looked at his grandfather and asked, "Grandpa, why did you ask me that?"

—Marcie Leitzke
Gresham, Wisconsin

OUR 2-year-old grandson, Thad, was riding on his grandfather's shoulders when he noticed his thinning hair.

"Papa," he asked, "why do you have so much skin in your hair?"

—Carla Warfield
Gaithersburg, Maryland

SINCE we have three full-grown Great Danes, we often need a dog sitter when we go away. This duty is usually filled by my son, his wife and their 4-year-old daughter, Ashlyn.

During our most recent vacation, Ashlyn—after

What did the pickle say when he wanted to play cards? "Dill me in."

what must have been a particularly trying day of letting the dogs in and out and hearing them bark—asked her mom, "Next time can't Grandma and Grandpa take the dogs on hibernation with them?"

—*Barbara Rich*
Orland, California

WE LIVE near a forest, and I often go for walks there, looking for deer with our 5-year-old granddaughter, Amy.

On one visit, we didn't see any deer as far as we went. Amy wanted to go deeper into the forest, so we did and were rewarded with the sighting of a deer.

Upon our return, I noticed Amy lagging behind. She was tired but refused to admit it.

When we came upon a field of wildflowers, Amy sat down and said, "C'mon, Grandpa, sit by me and watch the flowers grow."

—*Wendell Robinette*
Lockeford, California

MY GRANDDAUGHTER Emily and I were walking in from the barn one night.

BERRY GOOD. "Great-Grandpa Jack helped our son Kyle pick raspberries," says Tina Stevens, Sandpoint, Idaho.

I pointed out the moon, of which only a sliver was showing.

"I see it," she said, "but it's kinda turned off."

—*Edna Miller*
Fredericksburg, Ohio

OUR OLDEST daughter, Bonnie, was baby-sitting for a 6-week-old baby who was being fussy. Her son Brian, 4, finally said, "Mommy, should we go to Grandma's?"

"Why?" Bonnie asked.

"Well," replied Brian, "because she's a grandma

and she knows all about babies. You're just a mommy."
—*Virginia Bunce*
Corry, Pennsylvania

 I RECEIVED a call from our 7-year-old granddaughter, Reanne, who excitedly told me about the new "horse shoes" her mom had bought her for school.

When she described the shoes as being "white with a black thing in the middle", I realized she meant saddle shoes.
—*Marylynn Wrinkle*
Simi Valley, California

MY grandson's name is Henry John Hayes. So when he was 5, I asked if he'd like to be nicknamed Hank or Jake.

He replied, "I'd like to be called Junior."

"You can't be Junior," I told him. "Your dad's name is Charles."

"Yes, I can," he insisted. "I was born in June."
—*Bucky Foote*
Winston-Salem,
North Carolina

OUR 3-year-old granddaughter, Shelby, and her family were visiting us when her mother overheard her ask me for some money.

"Shelby," her mother said, "you know that you shouldn't ask people for money."

Shelby stepped back and said in a small voice, "I sure wish someone would offer me some!"
—*Nadyne Dickson*
Halsey, Oregon

OUR 3-year-old great-grandson, Joshua, was sitting next to his new baby sister. His aunt asked him if the baby was going to talk, and he replied that she couldn't.

When asked why not, he answered, "Because she doesn't have her batteries yet." —*Mrs. Barton Buss*
Chandler, Arizona

WHEN WE were preparing to leave our son's house to return home, our 3-year-old granddaughter was upset. I assured her we'd be flying back soon for another visit.

"Grandma," she said as

she started flapping her arms, "could you please teach me to fly, too?"
—*Nan Kaag*
Belleview, Florida

OUR 3-year-old grandson, Jordan, had been helping get the nursery ready for his expected baby sister. That evening Jordan put his head on his mom's stomach and said, "You can come out now. Your room's ready." —*Elaine Stone*
Roy, Utah

BIG SHOES TO FILL. Kaitlyn Byers, Hager City, Wis., loves to put on her dad's clothes, says Mom Roxanne.

AT THE AGE of 3, my granddaughter counted to 10 for us one night. My daughter-in-law then asked her if she could do it backwards. In response, she turned around, faced the wall and counted to 10 again! —*Viola Piper*
Rockland, Wisconsin

OUR 4-year-old grandson, Kyle, was trying to learn the difference between the words "tooth" and "teeth".

His mother told him if you have one, it's "tooth", and if you have two, they are "teeth". Then she asked him, "What would you say if you had three?"

Kyle thought for a moment, then he responded, "I'd have one tooth and two teeth." —*Joyce Breedlove*
East Lansing, Michigan

AFTER a snowfall, I asked my 4-year-old grandson what he was up to.

He said he had just built a snowman outside with his mom. Thinking it would soon melt, I asked him if he thought it would stay around for a while.

He responded, "Oh, yes,

Grandpa, we didn't put any 'feets' on him."
—*David Flory*
Frankfurt, Indiana

AMANDA, our 5-year-old granddaughter, has become pretty computer-literate since her family purchased a computer. So I asked her if they were on the World Wide Web yet. Amanda replied, "Oh, no. My mommy is afraid of spiders."
—*Mary Benbenek*
Fort Wayne, Indiana

JUST BEFORE Christmas, our 6-year-old grandson was staying with us overnight. He was learning to read and write, so he was sitting at a desk practicing his printing.

"Nana, I know what we are giving you and PapPap for Christmas," he said unexpectedly.

"That's nice," I replied. "But why don't you keep it a secret so you don't spoil the surprise."

"Oh, I won't tell," he re-sponded. "I just want to write myself a note about it." After a pause, he asked, "Nana, how do you spell gas grill?"   —*Jeanette Jeffries*
Harrisburg, Pennsylvania

AFTER a heavy snowstorm, I phoned our grandson, Alex, and asked him if he got about a foot of snow where he lived.

"More than a foot!" he exclaimed. "A whole leg!"
—*Carol Koetje*
McBain, Michigan

OUR granddaughter Brittany, 5, loves to visit our small farm. On one occasion, I was showing her old pictures of when our three children were small.

Later, Brittany asked, "Grandma, how come you didn't keep your kids?"
—*Pat Habiger*
Spearville, Kansas

GRANDDAUGHTER Ashley and I were discussing the new baby her family

How do you feel when you catch a firefly?
De-light-ful!

BUSY DAY. "My grandson Logan likes exploring his parents' acreage," says Linda Brockman, Chehalis, Wash.

was expecting in a few months.

Ashley, 4, explained, "If Mommy has two babies, we'll have twins. And if she has three babies, then we'll have *trumpets!*"

—*Mary McQuegge*
Columbia, Missouri

MY HUSBAND was looking at some old pictures with our grandson Ryan. One of the pictures showed my husband and his high school basketball team.

Ryan studied the picture for a minute and said, "Boy, Grandpa, basketball sure was invented a long time ago, wasn't it?" —*Pat Lane*
Pullman, Washington

SINCE my home is on the same acreage as my son's home, I see my four grandchildren frequently, especially the youngest, 4-year-old Amber.

One winter day, Amber came home with me for a visit. After I'd removed my snow boots, her eyes grew huge and a look of wonder came over her face.

"Grandma, your socks match!" she exclaimed with amazement.

—*Evelyn Cleal*
Lolo, Montana

WHILE visiting us, our 6-year-old granddaughter, Erica, saw her grandpa take his dentures out.

"Grandpa, you just took the smile right off your face," she said. Needless to say, we both had to smile at that one. —*Delta Shafar*
Newton, Kansas

I HEARD my granddaughter Lisa scream and ran to

see what was wrong. "Grandma, there's a spider on the table," she cried.

I took a look and told her, "That's not a spider, it's a daddy longlegs."

Lisa looked at me through tear-filled eyes and said, "Well, his *last name* is spider." —*Ruth Becker Warrenton, Missouri*

OUR granddaughter Sonya lives in southern California and was watching it snow for the first time.

"Oh, Grandma, what is it?" she said as she watched the flakes flutter down.

"That is snow, honey," I explained to her.

"Snow!" she shrieked. "Why, it looks like popped rain!" —*Lila Gross Alva, Oklahoma*

I HAVE a partial plate, and granddaughter Krista is always amazed when I remove my teeth to brush them.

Her other grandpa lives in Montana, and he takes her horseback riding when she visits there.

One night I phoned, and Krista's mother said, "It's Grandpa, and he wants to talk to you."

Krista said, "Is it the

NEEDS SOME REPAIRS. "Our grandson Brett thought his toy tractor needed some work done on it," say JoAnne and Orval Leistico from Elk River, Minnesota.

grandpa with the teeth or the one with the horse?"
—*Keith Ballantyne*
Ashland, Ohio

I WAS explaining to our granddaughter about what people do when they can't hear and see well.

"Folks wear hearing aids and glasses to help themselves," I told her.

Little Jennie then asked, "What do you do if you can't smell?"
—*Wanda Wiedemeier*
Porterfield, Wisconsin

ONE DAY our little granddaughter, Chelsea, asked her mother, "What day was I born?"

Her mother replied, "May 13, 1986."

A big smile came across Chelsea's face. "Hey, that's my birthday."
—*Helene Jenkins*
Quincy, Washington

GRANDSON Dennis, 3, was telling us about the cardinals he sees at his home in Virginia. When my husband took him out to the yard to fill the bird feed-

HARVEST HELPER. Matt Martin of Lariat, Texas is all smiles helping his dad, William, with the corn harvest.

ers, they spotted a blue jay.

"Look, Grandpa," Dennis said. "That cardinal is so cold he's turned blue."
—*Jackie Carney*
Augusta, Maine

I DIDN'T KNOW if my granddaughter had learned her colors yet, so I decided to test her. I'd point to something, ask her what color it was and she would tell me. We continued for a while until she looked at me and said, "Grandma, I really think you should try to figure out some of these yourself." —*Patricia Howard*
Rangely, Colorado

GOT EGGS? "Great-nephews Cody and Brady like exploring the chicken coop," says Lisa Mallmann, Hortonville, Wis.

The World Through The Eyes of a Child

Wit and wisdom from a kid's perspective.

ONE afternoon I was cooking when a strong earthquake struck. A large picture fell off the mantel and made a loud crash.

I panicked, ran to the bottom of the stairs and yelled my 4-year-old's name. He yelled back, "I didn't do it, Mom!"

—*Eirene Alexandrou*
San Jose, California

ONE LAZY afternoon, my 4-year-old daughter, Erin, and I were watching television.

Suddenly she made this observation: "I can tell that lady on TV doesn't have any kids...she's talking on the phone and she doesn't have her finger stuck in her ear!"

—*April Dusek*
Libby, Montana

WHEN my son was about 3 and would get into trouble, I'd call him with a stern voice—using both his first and his middle names. One day someone asked him what his first name was, and he replied, "Ryan."

When asked his middle name, he replied, "Christopher." Finally, the person asked his last name...and Ryan said, "Get over here!"

—*Linda Monteil*
Yukon, Oklahoma

WHEN two of our friends went outside to smoke, our 8-year-old son, Joey, informed them that smoking was unhealthy. He told them they should quit like his grandpa did.

They in turn asked how his grandpa quit, and Joey answered, "He ate cold turkey!"

—*Cindy Sands*
Racine, Ohio

ONE September evening, my husband was carrying our 5-year-old, Donnie, off to bed. When Donnie reached out to touch the thermostat, his daddy told him not to touch it.

"Why?" Donnie asked. "Will it change the weather?"

—*Karen Shoemaker*
Cochranville, Pennsylvania

Why do witches ride brooms?
Vacuum cleaners are too heavy.

MY great-niece Sheena, 5, had heard several times that Christmas was "just around the corner".

One afternoon, as she and her 3-year-old brother were excitedly looking out the window at the falling snow, she told him all about Christmas, ending with: "And you know, Jonathan, Christmas is only two blocks away!"

—*Nancy Maiden*
West Chicago, Illinois

AFTER dinner one night, I asked my 3-year-old,

LEAPIN' LIZARD! "My nephew Jamie ⊃uldn't take his eyes off this lizard," ⁄s Nancy Friend, Lynchburg, Va.

Catherine, if she'd like to drive to her grandpa and grandma's house for a quick visit. Naturally, she said yes, then gave me a big hug.

A bit bewildered, though, she looked me square in the eyes and said, "But, Mommy, I don't know how to drive!"   —*Denise Cole*
Forest Park, Ohio

ONE night when I was putting my 3-year-old son, Jacob, to bed, I raised his window to let in the fresh air. When I went in to check on him a little later, I noticed the window had been shut.

I proceeded to open it once more, but Jacob interrupted me, "No, Mommy, don't open the window. You're letting in the dark."

—*Trenna Furrh*
Bonham, Texas

I HAD just put my young son to bed and had been called to his bedroom for the umpteenth time. My patience had worn thin.

When I heard him call "Mama!" once again, I yelled back at him, "If you call 'Mama' one more time,

I'll spank you!"

After that it was quiet for a minute. Then I heard him call, in a voice just above a whisper, "Mrs. Green, may I have a drink?" —*Ellen Green Waukesha, Wisconsin*

 WHILE vacationing at Disney World and EPCOT Center, we struck up a conversation with a young family.

I said to their little boy, about 4 years old, "I'll bet you are having a fun time here at Disney World, aren't you?"

Wide-eyed with excitement, he said, "Yup! Tomorrow we're going to Apricot Center."

His mother kindly corrected him, "No, it's the EP-COT Center."

"That's what I told her, Mom," he repeated, "the Apricot Center!" —*Carol Young Great Falls, Montana*

MY 5-year-old son and I went into a pet shop. We were looking at all the cute puppies, one of which he wanted very much.

He asked me, "How much does that puppy cost?" I checked the price and replied, "$125."

He paused a moment, then looked at me very seriously and asked, "Do you think we could get a used one?" —*Barb Raymo Madison, Minnesota*

WHEN my son was about 2 years old, we visited my mother's and found that her older sister was there, too. Joe had never seen his great-aunt before, and he kept looking from one woman to the other. Finally he declared, "Grandmother, you and this girl look *like both of you!*" —*Bernice Mitchell Denton, Texas*

OUR SON'S teacher said he needed to work on following written directions. So I decided to let him practice by cooking according to a recipe.

He was enthusiastically making brownies one day when he called for my help. When I got to the kitcher

DEEP IN THOUGHT. "Nephews Jakob and Eli watched intently as a butterfly with an injured wing attempted to fly away," says Lois Huey from Rochester, Minn.

I was shocked to find his hands completely covered by chocolate mix.

"What are you *doing*?" I demanded.

"Just following directions," he pointed out innocently. "Step four says to mix by hand."—*Joan Smith, St. Marys, Pennsylvania*

MARTHA AND MARK were showing their son, Chad, their family photo album when he asked, "Who's that good-looking guy with the curly hair and big muscles?"

Martha answered, "Why, Chad, that's your father."

Chad looked at Mark and asked, "Then who is he?" — *Larry Tobin, Tomahawk, Wisconsin*

YEARS AGO, when my son Kevin was about 4, he was sitting on his bed coloring a picture.

I noticed the fringe on his bedspread needed to be "evened up", so I grabbed a pair of scissors and started trimming. I had done this a couple of other times after washing the bedspread.

Kevin looked at me and said, "That stuff sure grows

...st. You just cut it last week."
—*Mrs. James Madeiros*
Thousand Oaks, California

WE passed several horses in a field on the way to my parents' home one morning. Each of them was wearing a colorful blanket.

Our 3-year-old son exclaimed quickly, "Look, Mom. Those horses are still wearing their pajamas!"
—*Anne Wilson*
Parker, Colorado

MY 4-year-old son, Dallas, looked up at the cloudy sky and said, "Mommy, the sun isn't working today."
—*Loleita Wood*
Jefferson City, Missouri

MY 12-year-old daughter asked me for a baby picture of myself to use for a school project. I gave her one without thinking to ask what the project was about.

A few days later, I was in her classroom for a par-ent-teacher meeting, when I noticed my picture pinned to a mural the students had created. The title of their project was "The Oldest Things in My House".
—*Alma Catgott*
Round Rock, Texas

ON THE way home from taking our daughters, Jennifer, 5, and Sarah, 2, to the movies, Jennifer asked me, "Mom were we at 'A Theater Near You'?"
—*Jo Boring*
Silver Lake, Indiana

ONE DAY my son and my niece climbed on the roof of the house. She was afraid to climb down.

It sure got my attention when my son told her to just "fall off".

"It's better to have a broken arm than to live up there!" he explained.
—*Lois Shenold*
Littleton, Colorado

AN ANNUAL dog census is taken where we live. Last

Would you like to hear a joke about a jump rope? No, just skip it.

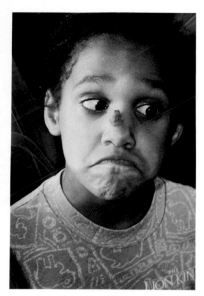

BEING NOSY. "Granddaughter Chelsea looked funny with a frog on her nose," says Cathy Reits, Grand Rapids, Mich.

friend said to Bryan.

"Oh, no," Bryan replied. "We brought him with us!"
—*Mary Rumans*
Versailles, Missouri

I WAS rushing around the house one morning and my girls were sitting on my bed, still in their pajamas. I told them to get dressed because it was getting late.

My 5-year-old, Amanda, looked outside and said, "Mom, it's not late—if it was late it would be nighttime!" —*Sandra Pierce*
El Paso, Texas

time the census-taker came by, our 5-year-old daughter, Katie, answered the door.

"Little girl, does your doggie have a license?" she was asked.

Katie shook her head "No," she said. "My 'Princess' doesn't even drive!"
—*Patricia Campbell*
Orange, California

AT A Fourth of July picnic a friend was asking our 4-year-old, Bryan, about his little baby brother.

"I hear you have a new baby at your house," the

AFTER boarding a train on route from our son's house, we were given a seat that faced the rear of the train.

My 4-year-old son appraised the situation for a minute and said, "Mom, they must have put the batteries in backwards!"
—*Mrs. C.K. Smucker*
Coatesville, Pennsylvania

AFTER telling my 7-year-old niece I was planning a surprise birthday party for her grandma, I reminded the youngster not to tell

Grandma about the party.

My niece promptly asked, "You mean Grandma doesn't know it's her birthday?" —*Pat Sowinski Chicago, Illinois*

I WAS baking cookies one day when one of my little neighbor friends came over for a visit. He sat silently for a little while, then said, "My stomach is talking to me."

"What is it saying?" I asked.

He replied, "My stomach is telling me that you bake the best cookies of anyone in the whole world."

—*Bonnie Baumgardner Sylva, North Carolina*

WHEN our son Jeff was 3, he saw some suckers at the store and asked for one. I said, "No, we're broke and can't afford to buy candy."

The following week we were in the same store, and Jeff asked, "Mommy, are we fixed yet?"—*Bette Reuland Montgomery, Illinois*

SEVERAL MONTHS ago, we adopted a golden re-

FEATHERED FRIENDS. "Son Michael was intrigued by these baby chicks," says Ruby Shoup, Millersburg, Ohio.

triever-collie mix dog from the animal shelter. Recently, I purchased a different brand of dog food than we normally buy.

Looking at the bag, which featured a picture of a dalmatian, my 5-year-old daughter asked with great concern. "Mom, if 'Sugar' eats this, will she turn into a dalmatian?" —*Ann Bolick Hemet, California*

YEARS AGO, I baby-sat for a small boy. One day we had a terrible hailstorm that really scared him.

I picked him up, opened

up the garage door and watched the hail bounce across the driveway. He put his arms around my neck and asked, "Why is it raining ice cubes?"

—*Doris Frank*
Randolph, New York

JONATHAN, our 2-year-old, was in a store with me when a friend came in with her daughter Shelby. I introduced her saying, "Jonathan, this is Shelby."

Jonathan got so busy looking at toys he didn't notice when my friend and the little girl left. Minutes later, another woman came in with a daughter about the same age. I was surprised to learn the girl had the same name.

When I brought her over and said, "Jonathan, this is Shelby", he studied her and got a puzzled look on his face. He turned to me and said, "Mommy, she changed faces!"—*Juli Ellis*
Lees Summit, Missouri

OUR neighbors' little boy is learning to dress himself. When his mother told him e had his shoes on the

wrong feet, he looked puzzled and replied, "But these are the only feet I have."

—*Katie Barnes*
Pearland, Texas

OUR 4-year-old son, Scott, was out with his grandparents and passed a pond that usually had geese swimming there. Well, that day there weren't any geese.

"Grandma, where are all the geese today?" Scott asked.

"It's getting cold, so they probably flew to Florida." Grandma replied.

They drove along and saw another pond with geese on it. That's when Scott asked, "Grandma, is that Florida?"

—*Crystal Lamb*
Waynesville, Ohio

OUR SON Trent, who is 2, knows he's done something wrong when we call out his full name, Trent Alan Noel, in a loud stern voice.

One particular day our dog "Sparky" was jumping on Trent and licking his face. "Get down!" Trent or-

KITTY KISS. "Our son Austin puckered up for a smooch with Grandma's little kitten," says Lana Smith from Enoch, Utah.

dered. When Sparky continued to jump up, Trent put his hands on his hips and said loudly, "Get down, Sparky Alan Dog!"
—*Tom and Katie Noel Harlem, Montana*

OUR daughter Casey went to whisper something into her dad's ear. Immediately our son Keith went to his dad's other ear.

"I'm going to listen," he explained. —*Judy Queen Trinity, North Carolina*

AMBER, our 4-year-old daughter, likes to watch for the milkman because he makes deliveries in a truck painted like a Holstein.

One day, she noticed a plain brown UPS truck in front of our house. She quickly ran to get me and exclaimed, "Mom, the chocolate milkman's here! Let's buy some."
—*Mrs. Garth Huddleston Renton, Washington*

IN 1973, my husband and I decided to move from a small town in Maryland to Seattle, Washington. We spent a lot of time discussing the trip with our son and daughter, wh were 11 and 6 at the time.

Both children were excited and talked about going to Seattle all the way during our 3,000-mile journey. On the last day of our trek, we stopped to eat breakfast.

When we told the kids we were only 100 miles from Seattle, our daughter piped up, "Mom, who is Attle?" —*H.M. Stoneburner Maxwelton, West Virginia*

ONE EVENING, I asked our 4-year-old son, Andy, to pick up his toys and crayons.

Ordinarily, this was a rather drawn-out process. This time, however, was different. When I looked in to see how Andy was progressing, I found everything in its appropriate place.

He glanced up at me and said, "That was a novelty, wasn't it?"

—*Richard Washburn Vacaville, California*

AFTER VOTING at our local polling place, I was leaving with my 3-year-old daughter, Elizabeth. She asked when I was going to vote, so I told her I just did.

She replied, "But you never raised your hand once." —*Sharon Peterson Lincoln, Nebraska*

MY son brought home a picture of Noah's Ark that he had drawn in kindergarten. It was lovely, but I asked him why he'd colored the elephants green.

"Because they're seasick," he explained.

—*Jean Becker Redford, Michigan*

MY DAUGHTER watched with interest as a young woman tried unsuccessfully to calm her crying infant.

As the baby continued to fuss, my daughter leaned over to me and whispered, "I think the lady just got the baby. She hasn't learned how to work it yet!" —*Betsy Zenk, Lakota, Iowa*

JUST BEFORE returning from a visit to my folks' house, my 3-year-old son, Paul, had been with Grandpa on his front porch, looking at the night sky.

Paul slept most of the way during the 2-hour journey home. When he awoke and got out of the car, he looked at the sky and yelled delightedly, "The moon followed us home!"

—*Patricia Butler*
Kent, Washington

MY BROTHER'S granddaughter Rachel, 6, visited us a while back. She fell in love with our two basset hounds, "Sam" and "Susie".

Later, Rachel asked her mom what relation she is to the people with the dogs. Her mom explained that our daughter, Teresa, is Rachel's second cousin.

"Well," Rachel said, "I guess that makes me third cousin to the dogs."

—*Nina Hudgens*
North Little Rock, Arkansas

WHEN I walked into the bathroom to put away towels, I discovered the light bulb had burned out. It wasn't real dark so I went about my business, forgetting to change the bulb.

Later, when my 5-year-old daughter, Nicole, went into the bathroom and turned on the switch, she came out running and exclaimed, "Mommy, come quick, we ran out of electricity in the bathroom!"

—*Laurie Hayse*
Indianapolis, Indiana

OUR friends' 4-year-old daughter, Elysse, was going for her first horseback riding lesson. After getting on the horse, Elysse was handed the reins.

"Could you tell me what these are for?" the instructor asked.

"Of course," Elysse replied. "They're the brakes!" —*Courtney Frye*
Danville, Kentucky

MY NIECE Amy and her husband, Bill, had two daughters, Kelsey, 4, and Erica, 2, and were expecting their third girl. So Bill explained to Kelsey that

Why did the chicken cross the playground?
It wanted to get to the other slide.

WRENCHING EXPERIENCE. "My husband, Ken, was fixing a car when our grandson Timmy grabbed a wrench to lend a hand," says Sandra Mitchell, Villa Ridge, Mo.

she would be getting a new little sister soon.

When Kelsey started to cry, Bill asked her what was wrong. "I don't want a new little sister," Kelsey sobbed. "I like Erica."

—*Natalie Blair*
Nutley, New Jersey

ONE DAY I spotted my son Keith, 3 at the time, standing in the front hall holding the screen door open.

"Close the door," I told him. "You're letting all the flies in."

He turned to me with a ᴘuzzled look on his face and said, "No, I'm not, Mom. I'm letting them out!"

—*Dorothy Steinert*
Long Beach, California

MY BROTHER Austin and his 5-year-old daughter, Julia, were heading out early in the morning, and there was dew all over the grass and car. Thinking that Julia had probably never heard the word "dew" before, Austin asked her if she knew what that water was called.

She replied matter-of-factly, "Condensation."

Austin had to hold back

his laughter when he told her that was correct, and then added that some people simply call it "dew".

—Heather Ceiley
Anaheim Hills, California

MY FRIEND'S 3-year-old daughter was very eager for Christmas to arrive and was constantly asking when it would come.

The mother's standard answer was, "It's right around the corner." One day the little girl got fed up and replied, "Which corner, Mommy? I keep looking, but I can't find it."

—Lucy Dimas
Lordsburg, New Mexico

OUR 5-year-old daughter wanted a pet, so my husband and I started looking for a dog that was already "house trained".

We finally found one, and the next day I overheard Jodi on the telephone describing every detail about her new dog.

Then she added in a sad voice, "But guess what, Jan. My puppy's house is broken!" *—Arti Stewart*
England, Arkansas

DRINK UP. "Grandkids Lisa and Katie like watering flowers and themselves," says Mary Jane Swihart, Quinter, Kan.

AFTER being away all winter, my rapidly growing nephew, Nanue, returned to the camp that his Grandpa Bob and Grandma June operate during the summer. He turned to them and said, "Grandpa, you lowered the bunks!"*—Lori Vial*
Commerce Township,
Michigan

MY HUSBAND and I were up early one morning and opted for coffee on the patio. It was foggy, and we could barely see the pasture behind the house.

My mom, who was visi‑

ing, came out with our 3-year-old, Hannah. Still sleepy-eyed, Hannah looked around and said, "Oh, no, Grandma. The clouds have fallen down."
—*Beth Campbell*
Hardin, Texas

MY SON, who was 2 years old at the time, intently watched me make his bed. As I was struggling to put the fitted sheet over the mattress corner, he said, "You need a shoehorn, Mom." —*Mina Scheuerman*
Camdenton, Missouri

WHEN my mother-in-law phoned, our 4-year-old daughter, Sara, answered and talked to "Maw Maw" until I got on the line.

When her grandmother asked what time her daddy would be home from work, Sara quipped, "When dinner is ready."
—*Jodi Leathers*
Pasadena, Maryland

EMILY, my 3-year-old niece, watched as her mother took a carton of eggs from the dairy case. Open-ing the carton to check for broken ones, her mom let Emily inspect them, too.

They were brown eggs—something Emily had not seen before. Emily let out a sigh and said, "Oh, they're not ripe yet."
—*Elizabeth Harper*
Santa Barbara, California

MY 6-year-old son was looking for his kitten. He looked under the bed, but since it was dark under there, he got a flashlight.

"Look, Mom!" he said, shining the light on the kitten. "She's under there, and she turned her headlights on!" —*Nancy Jacobs*
DeKalb, Illinois

I WAS TALKING to my 3-year-old son, Stephen, about the U.S. Presidents and taught him the names of our country's first and current President.

That evening when my husband came home from work, I asked Stephen if he could tell his dad who the first President was.

Looking at us with a great big smile, he proudly said, "George Washing Machine." —*Anita Jackson Summerville, South Carolina*

ONE DAY my daughters, Shelby, 9, and Kelsey, 6, were playing wedding. In the role as the minister, Shelby said to Kelsey, "Now repeat your vows after me."

To which Kelsey, the miniature bride, replied, "I don't have to repeat them. I already know them: A-E-I-O-U." —*Mary Miller Elizabeth, Indiana*

AS I was putting my two young sons to bed one night, I asked them, "Of all the little boys in the whole wide world, how did I get the very best two?"

Michael, who is 4, got a big smile on his face and said, "You must have picked the right seeds." —*Diane Long Phoenix, Arizona*

WHILE OUT for a walk with his dad one day, my 4-year-old nephew, Stevie, spotted a white poodle up ahead.

He began to run after the dog, but his dad stopped him and reminded him not to chase after strange dogs.

Stevie said, "But, Dad, that's not a dog—it's a sheep!"

It was the first poodle Stevie had seen. —*Cindy Paris Hilton, New York*

THE EVENING after we waxed our car, it rained. The next morning, our son, Austin, 4, saw the rainwater beaded on the newly waxed finish and said, "Mom, the car has goose bumps." —*Sherry Goins Mt. Vernon, Ohio*

HAVING just moved to the country, my family and I sure enjoyed the views. A real treat were the rainbows.

We didn't realize how much our 2-year-old son, P.J., took rainbow watching to heart, until he pointed out a bruise on his leg.

"Look, Mommy," he said. "I have a rainbow on my leg." —*Tim Duff Spokane, Washington*

SPLASHDOWN. "It stopped raining, so Morgan went out to play. I had my camera ready as she jumped into a puddle," says her dad, Rick Goette, Milledgeville, Ga.

MY 3-year-old son, Daniel, reluctantly agreed to spend a few days with Grandma and Grandpa. As they were riding in the car to their house, he passed the time by looking through Grandma's purse.

When he asked what some pills were, she explained she took them to keep from getting carsick.

He immediately asked, "Do you have any pills to keep me from getting homesick?" —*Sharon York Albion, Illinois*

WHEN my cousin's wife was expecting her third child, her 3- and 4-year-old

Why did the elephant run away from the circus? He was tired of working for peanuts.

girls followed her around, constantly asking questions.

One day they asked her how she got jars of baby food in her tummy to feed the baby.

When they were told the baby didn't eat like that and was just sleeping, they incredulously asked, "You mean you have a crib in there, too?"

—*Marietta Cordell*
Myrtle Beach, South Carolina

MY friend's son always requested a rabbit for Christmas, and was disappointed when he never got one. Last year, he surprised his mom and asked for a magic wand and a magician's hat.

When she asked why, he replied, "So I can pull a rabbit out of the hat."

—*Eliza Anderson*
Paris, Michigan

WHENEVER MY 3-year-old son misbehaved, I asked him, "Where is my sweet little boy?"

I didn't realize what an impression this was making until one afternoon when we were riding in the

OPEN WIDE. "Richard Wigfield enjoyed visiting during strawberry season," says Grandma Olive Foss, Badger, Minn.

car and he kept misbehaving in the backseat.

After scolding him a number of times, I was shocked when I heard him ask, "Where is my sweet little mamma?"

—*Donna Williford*
Thomson, Georgia

AFTER HER first trip through an automatic car wash, 3-year-old daughter, Rayjeana, looked wide-eyed

at her dad and said, "That sure was a bad storm!"
—*Margie Bowie*
Aberdeen, Ohio

A WOMAN walked up to my little niece, Ashley, in a store and said, "Hello there, pretty miss, how old are you?"

"I'm 4," said Ashley.

"And when will you be 5?" the lady asked.

"When I get done being 4," said Ashley.
—*Lori Roseman*
Greendale, Wisconsin

WHILE DRIVING along the road next to the Ohio Canal, I was explaining to my 5-year-old how mules were used to pull boats down the canal many years ago.

He looked at me for a moment with a puzzled stare, then asked, "Didn't they drown?" —*Chet Ziniewicz*
Spencer, Ohio

MY SON wanted to play outside on his third birth-day. It was quite cold, so I bundled him up first.

Our neighbor saw him and went out to wish him a happy birthday. "How old are you now?" she asked.

After thinking for a minute, he responded, "I can't tell you because I've got my mittens on!"
—*Sandy Baxter*
Frankfort, Illinois

AFTER ripping into a Christmas present, 3-year-old Rebecca picked up the toy and said, "I've wanted one of these since I was a little girl!" —*Sudie Laney*
Centre, Alabama

OUR CAR stalled just as we pulled into the parking lot of the supermarket where we were going to buy groceries.

Our 7-year-old son, Kyle, looked at his dad and said, "This car is smart, Daddy. It knew to stop before you even shut it off."
—*JoAnne Fisher*
Lawrenceburg, Tennessee

Where do sheep get their hair cut?
At the baa-baa shop.

IS IT MY TURN? "Jake was watching a horse show in Crown Point," says his mom, Julie Alger from Hebron, Indiana.

It's time for a recess
from readin', writin'
and 'rithmetic.

I WAS helping a group of preschoolers make valentine hearts and asked the children the names of family members to write on their hearts.

When I asked one little girl the name of her dad, she told me she would have to think a bit.

After a while, she came back and said very seriously, "I got it! My daddy's name is Honey!"

—AbaGail Hills
Eden Prairie, Minnesota

MY GREAT-GRANDSON, 5-year-old Dustin, spent a week with us. When his parents picked him up, they explained that this would be his last visit before school.

As they pulled away, Dustin cried loudly. They asked him what was wrong, and he tearfully answered, "This is the last time I get to see Grandma and Grandpa till after college!"   *—Maxine Haltom*
Alden, Kansas

MY great-grandson John, 4, was at the day care center when a tornado warning was issued. The teacher ushered everyone into the basement.

When John's mother arrived to pick him up, she asked him why he was in the basement.

"We're down here because there's a vicious tomato coming," he answered matter-of-factly.

—Mrs. Robert Bremer
Carlinville, Illinois

AFTER returning from his first day at school, our son complained, "That bus driver was lost. He just drove around and around and *finally* found the school!"
—A.L. Wynn, Dayton, Ohio

HILARY, our granddaughter, told her kindergarten teacher that her dad was coming back that day from a business trip to Japan.

"Do you think your daddy will bring back something from Japan for you?" the teacher asked.

Hilary thought for a moment, then answered, "Oh, yes, a lot of dirty laundry."
—Beatrice Woodward
Southampton, New York

MY GRANDCHILDREN got a puppy, and their mother told them it had to be neutered. She asked if they knew what that meant.

"Oh, I know what that is," said 7-year-old Sam. "That's when you have to stay after school and let the teacher help you with your lessons." —*Eloise Brock*
Cheraw, South Carolina

OUR 7-year-old daughter was running during recess. When she suddenly sat down under the slide, her teacher came up to her and asked if she was okay.

"I just lost my breath," our daughter replied.

Her concerned teacher asked if that had ever happened before.

"Yes," our daughter answered, "but I found it the last time." —*Lynne Stinson*
Auburn, Kentucky

AT MY SON'S school, the children were encouraged to wear something green for St. Patrick's Day.

That morning the teachers asked how many of the children were Irish, and how many were German, Italian, French, etc. After my

CATCHING SOME ZZZ'S. "This is how our son Alex passes the time while our sow, 'Millie', eats her supper," says Phyllis Buffington from Luning, Nebraska.

son told me this, I asked him when he put his hand up.

"I never did," he answered. "She didn't ask for Americans." —*Anne Rhule Odenton, Maryland*

AT PRESCHOOL, the teacher was reading a story about a mystery. A little girl raised her hand to say she didn't understand what that meant.

"Does anyone know what we mean by a mystery?" the teacher asked the class.

My 4-year-old granddaughter, Lucy, raised her hand. "A mystery is when someone colors on the table, but no one knows who did it."
—*David Lincicome Issaquah, Washington*

WHEN MY son was in first grade, he came home one day and told me he'd had a substitute teacher. I asked him, "Was she a young woman or an older woman?"

He thought about this for a second and said, "I don't know. She looked brand-new to me."
—*Inez Murphy Galt, California*

I'M the office secretary for an elementary school. One day a teacher sent a little first grader to the office.

"Mr. T said my lip is bleeding, and I should go to the office to get some gasoline for it," she said.
—*Ellen Hastings Gill, Massachusetts*

OUR 5-year-old son came home from school with his school photo and disgustedly tossed it on the dining room table.

"Mom," he told me, "I had a big smile, but they just didn't put it in there."
—*Carolee Robie Roach, Missouri*

MY GRANDDAUGHTER, Stephanie, and her mother were at the store and ran

What kind of house weighs the least?
A lighthouse.

PUCKER UP. "My daughter Allie gave my parents' horse 'Joey' a big kiss one day," says Paula Falk, Hawley, Minn.

into Stephanie's kindergarten teacher. When Stephanie told me later on about her mother's visit with the teacher, I asked, "Were they talking about you?"

Stephanie thought for a moment, then replied, "I don't know...they were talking in cursive."

—*Clovis DeMent*
Rector, Arkansas

THE time was drawing near for our 5-year-old, Erin, to be tested at our local school, a process called, "kindergarten screening".

To prepare for this special day, we quizzed her every evening at the dinner table, asking questions like: "What's your phone number?" and "Can you count to 20?"

When we started asking questions the night before the screening, tears began to roll down Erin's cheeks. She said she didn't want to go to school.

We were shocked. When we asked her why, she replied, "I just know I won't like kindergarten screaming!"

—*Janet Moore*
Ogdensburg, New York

My sister was writing a letter, and her 2-year-old grandson decided he wanted to write one, too.

She gave him a sheet of paper and he busily made a number of marks on it and then, very businesslike, handed it to her.

"What does it say?" she asked him.

"I don't know," he said thoughtfully. "I can't read."

—*Irene Lynn*
Smithfield, Pennsylvania

CURIOUS about grandson Jason's first day at school, I

A REAL HANDFUL. "Emily likes to play with our kittens," says Grandma Lea Ann Brown, Mt. Pleasant, Texas.

asked him what he had learned.

"Not enough, Grandma," he replied solemnly. "I have to go back tomorrow."
—Pauline Wheeler
Montezuma, Iowa

WHEN our son Bob was in first grade, the students were having difficulty reading in front of the class one day. The teacher, Mrs. Webster, got up and said, "Now this is the way I expect you to read."

She opened the book and started reading slowly and evenly. Bob stood up and said, "No wonder Mrs. Webster can read so good—look how long she's been in first grade." *—Eleanor Olek*
Wayne, New Jersey

OUR THIRD grade was taking a state achievement test. One little girl raised her hand, and my fellow teacher went over to ask if she had a problem.

"Yes, I do," replied the little girl in a worried tone. "I don't understand this one question."

"Read it to me," whispered the teacher.

"It says, 'How many feet are in a yard?' " the little girl replied. "But it doesn't say *which* yard—the front or the back." *—Al Spencer*
Jonesboro, Arkansas

ONE DAY as my kindergarten class was getting ready to go home, one of my young students looked down at his feet.

"Oh, no!" he exclaimed.

When I asked what was wrong, he didn't say anything at first. Then he looked at me, shrugged his shoulders and pointed down to his shoes—which were on the wrong feet.

"Guess my legs got mixed up today," he said with a shrug.

—*Fran Haack*
Whiting, Iowa

EVERY MORNING, my friend's mother would call upstairs to wake up her and her sibilings.

"Kevin, get up! David, get up! Kimberley, get up! Sarah, get up!" she would, say, calling each of the kids' names from youngest to oldest.

When little Kevin started kindergarten, the teacher asked him what his name was. "Kevin," he replied. "And what is your last name, Kevin?" she asked. "Getup!" he answered proudly.

—*Rosemary Johnson*
Moose Jaw, Saskatchewan

I HAD TRIED to explain to my 6-year-old daughter how the days get shorter as winter approaches.

She apparently got the concept—sort of. One day in December, she rushed in from recess and told her teacher, "The days aren't the only things getting shorter—so are the recesses!" —*Jeanne Zornes*
Wenatchee, Washington

FOR HALLOWEEN, my daughter's preschool class had a costume party. While searching for the perfect accent for her witch costume, I told her I had a cute little broom she could take to school.

Slightly annoyed, she responded, "Oh, Mom, can't you just drive me there?"

—*Karen Lake*
Coldwater, Michigan

THERE was a party at our daughter's preschool, and I reminded her to be careful not to ruin her new dress.

When I went to pick her up after school, I saw her running and climbing with the other kids.

"Kate, did I see you

What allows you to see through walls?
A window.

climbing in your brand-new dress?" I asked as we drove home.

"I don't know, Mom," she replied. "Where were you parked?"
—*Mary Cauley*
St. Augustine, Florida

MY 4-year-old granddaughter had just learned to spell a few simple words at preschool. She was very excited when she told her mother, "Amy's mother has the same name as you…M-O-M!"
—*Joyce Bridgman*
Avon, Connecticut

I TOLD our 4-year-old son I was going to enroll him in school. He said, "Mom, I don't want to roll in school. I want to walk in."
—*Mary Parrett*
Menominee, Michigan

IN OUR school, we often hear over the intercom, "Will the janitor please page the office".

A little boy in our daughter's kindergarten class very seriously said to his teacher, "I hope they don't call my name. I don't know how to paint the office."
—*Ruth Cook*
Pascoag, Rhode Island

MY SON, William, 9, brought a note home from his teacher stating that William had not finished his homework. He was to bring back a written reason for not having done the work, signed by a parent.

William asked me what he should write. I said, "I think you should just write, 'I was too lazy.'"

William, his eyes now wide open, replied, "Mom, I can't write that!"

"Well, I think that is exactly what you should write," I responded.

The next morning, just before he left for school, William came to me with the note and said, "You have to sign this."

I took the time to look at it first, and he'd written, "My mom was too lazy."
—*Anne Marie Pelkofer*
Hales Corners, Wisconsin

WHEN our granddaughter Bekah was in first grade, her phonics teacher asked the students to verbalize the short vowel sounds of words. The teacher wrote dog on the board, and a boy made the short "o" sound.

When it was Bekah's turn, the teacher wrote cat on the board. And Bekah replied, "Meow!"

—*Janet Holden*
Lynchburg, Ohio

MY HUSBAND, Rick, was doing some paperwork on the kitchen table. Our 5-year-old daughter, Rosie, brought out a math paper and asked, "Daddy, why do I have to learn this dumb math stuff?"

He answered, "Honey, math is something you'll use your whole life. In fact, I'm using it right now in my work."

Her eyes got real big, and she quickly asked, "You mean you have to count the apples, too?"

—*Wendy Joseph*
Cincinnati, Ohio

WHEN our son Brian was about 2, I started helping him learn the ABC's.

He was doing very well until we reached the letter "W". I pronounced it for him, but he looked at me a little puzzled. I repeated it slower.

After thinking for a moment, his eyes twinkled and he said with a big grin, "Double Brian!"

—*Charlotte Brodie*
Mission Hills, California

MY 6-year-old daughter, Ashley, was learning to write simple sentences in

TREE HUGGER. Daniel Hentschl had fun playing at his Uncle Neal's country place near Harbor Beach, Mich.

A LONG WALK OFF A SHORT PIER. "My sister and I enjoy visiting our friends' farm and going swimming in their pond," says Melissa Hemken from Alden, Iowa.

school. She explained to me that the first word in a sentence always starts with a big letter.

"What does a sentence end with?" I asked her.

She looked at me for a while, then said, "A pimple."   —*Diane May Grayson, Louisiana*

I DIDN'T realize how much my 3-year-old son, Christopher, loved farming until his first day of preschool.

When the teacher held up a flash card for the color red, Christopher shouted, "International!" And when she held up a green

card, he yelled, "John Deere!"   —*Wendi Harrel Carthage, Illinois*

WHEN MY identical twin daughters were in kindergarten, a young boy saw them walking down the hall. He went running to his teacher and exclaimed, "Teacher, come here quick! There are two girls out here and they both have the same face on!"

—*Peggy Grice Hazelwood, North Carolina*

EMILY, our 5-year-old niece, often follows her dad

around the farm asking a lot of questions.

One day in kindergarten, the teacher was talking about manners. "What do you do when you break something?"

Emily quickly responded, "Go to town to get parts!" —*Elizabeth Weber*
Dimock, South Dakota

I WAS ENJOYING the lively company of my neighbor's granddaughter. When I asked her how old she was, she held up four fingers and replied, "This many."

Then, her brown eyes sparkling with excitement, she held up her thumb along with the four fingers. "And when I go to kindergarten, I'll be a handful!"

—*Louisa Pilkington*
Smithfield, Illinois

WHEN OUR grandson, Brad, was small, he loved to have someone read to him and was also very eager to learn how to read himself.

His parents told him he'd learn how to read when he went to school. After the first day of school, they were surprised to see him crying.

"What's the matter?" his mother asked. Brad replied, "I went to school and I *still* can't read!"

—*George Flege*
Lockland, Ohio

EACH YEAR as her three older siblings marched off to kindergarten after their fifth birthdays, my granddaughter Danielle had watched attentively.

Finally, she, too, turned 5. When someone told her enthusiastically that soon she would be a schoolgirl, she burst into tears.

"I don't want to go to school," she sobbed. "My teeth will start falling out!"

—*Esther Williams*
Richfield, Utah

ONE of my grandsons came home from his first day at school and announced he wasn't going back.

When his mom asked why not, he replied, "I can't read, I can't write and they won't let me talk!"

—*Janett Curtis*
Brasher Falls, New York

HAPPY COWPOKE. "My son Chance grinned widely when I took this photo," says Sheila Leach, Douglas, Wyoming.

Just What the Doctor Ordered

This will cure
whatever ails you—
if you don't split
your insides laughing.

AFTER missing a day of school, 6-year-old Melinda proudly showed her teacher her shiny new filling and announced, "I went with Mommy to the dentist yesterday and had my tooth welded!"
—*Merle Sheffer*
Seneca, Pennsylvania

SIZING UP THE CATCH. "Sons Kord and Tek are best fishing buddies," says Yvonne Cackley, Yellville, Ark.

KAYLA, our 4-year-old granddaughter, had been to the doctor before she came to visit us. So when she saw Papaw (her grandpa) resting on the sofa, she wanted to play nurse. She pretended to take his temperature, covered him with a blanket and asked him how he was feeling.

Then Kayla asked Papaw, who was half asleep, to stick out his finger. "This won't hurt a bit," she said as she proceeded to draw blood with a straight pin from my pincushion.

Papaw jumped up from the couch in a hurry!
—*Madonna McCauley*
Cox's Creek, Kentucky

WHEN OUR son Caleb was 6, we took him with us to visit a relative in the hospital. I explained that it was the same hospital where he was born.

As we were visiting, a nurse came in to check on the patient. Our son piped up, "Hi, I'm Caleb. Remember me?"
—*Jane Knisely*
Imler, Pennsylvania

SHORTLY after Frank, my second-grader grandson, had studied the body's internal organs in health class, his parents were listening to a Christian radio station. The speaker on the radio was talking about the

New Testament.

A few minutes into the program, Frank informed his parents, "We learned about the small intestament and the large intestament, but the teacher never told us about the new intestament."—*Bonnie Reiter*
Yakima, Washington

MY NIECE, who was expecting her fifth child, had a doctor's appointment and took two of her youngsters along. One of the children asked, "Are we going to see if the baby is done?"
—*Ruth Simpson*
Gretna, Virginia

MY grandson, Daniel, who is 3, proved that kids usually take things literally and can often come up with a whole different meaning than what was intended.

While at the doctor's office for his annual physical, Daniel was having his physical coordination checked.

The doctor asked Daniel, "Can you jump on one foot?"

Daniel shrugged his shoulders, looked at the doctor with a what-the-heck-he-asked-for-it expression, and then took a mighty jump for his size and landed on the doctor's foot!   —*Jeanne Lotz*
Milwaukee, Wisconsin

GRANDSON Charley, recovering from chicken pox, was able to play outside but was still covered with many spots. He was in the backyard when his mother told him to avoid the mosquitoes.

"Don't worry, they won't bite me, Mom…I'm all used up!"   —*Mary White*
River Forest, Illinois

ONE DAY, our 3-year-old son asked me to lie on his bed and pretend to be his patient.

While he was getting his doctor's kit together, he heard something on the television in the other room

---

Why did the foal cough?
He was feeling a little horse.

and left to see what it was.

"What about me?" I called out.

"I'll be back in just a minute," he said from the other room. "I need to check on some other patients."

—Vicki Terry
Lawton, Michigan

OUR daughter was 3 and had an eye infection, so we took her to the doctor.

A nurse was instructed to put salve in Johanna's eye. When she was finished, she told our daughter, "Bat your eye now."

Apparently Johanna did not exactly understand what the nurse meant. She hesitated just a moment— then "batted" herself in the eye with her tiny hand!

—Joann White
Thayer, Kansas

WHEN MY cousin Mendy was in the hospital, her doctor placed her on a liquid diet. He explained that she could eat anything she could hold up to the light and see through.

Mendy asked hopefully, "A doughnut?"

—Andrea Murray
Tecumseh, Oklahoma

AFTER receiving a fluoride treatment during a visit to the dentist, our 4-year-old grandson came home and proudly informed us that he had "Florida" on his teeth. —Thomas Lapham
Flint, Michigan

MY DAUGHTER Janis, 6, came down with chicken pox, and as I applied lotion to the rash on her stomach, her 2-year-old sister, Louisa, was watching. Louisa wasn't sick, but not to be outdone by her older sibling, she raised her shirt and asked, "Mommy, will you rub my chicken parts, too?" —Bonita Umberger
Hamburg, Pennsylvania

WHEN MY son Jamey was 3, his Aunt Linda entered the hospital and came

Why is it easy to weigh fish?
They all have their own scales.

SHINING STARS. "Our daughters, Taylor, Danielle and Katie, had the patriotic spirit during a Fourth of July celebration," says Natalie Klessens of Modesto, Calif.

home with a baby. Six weeks later, I went to the hospital and returned with a baby brother for Jamey. About 3 months later, Jamey's great-grandma and grandpa were admitted to the hospital. As I was telling my husband the news, Jamey got excited and said, "Oh boy, two more babies!" —*Janet Moser Paola, Kansas*

MY GRANDSON Kenny was visiting me when his Aunt Teri stopped by. Kenny asked if his two cousins could come over to play, but Teri explained that they had been exposed to the chicken pox and shouldn't visit Kenny.

After thinking a moment, Kenny said, "But Aunt Teri, they won't get chicken pox because you don't have any chickens." —*Shirley Buckner Paris, Illinois*

WHEN my granddaughter Lindsay, who was 8, had the flu, the doctor told her to drink plenty of fluids so she would not get dehydrated. When her dad asked Lindsay what the doctor had said, she replied, "He told Mommy to keep me moist so I won't evaporate."—*Janie Gilmore Elgin, Texas*

MY youngest brother was about 4 years old when he caught the chicken pox. He wanted to see himself in the mirror, and after looking at his reflection for several minutes, he started crying.

When Mother asked him what was wrong, he replied in between sobs, "I don't have any feathers."
—*Mrs. R.L. Nelson Jr. Hot Springs, Virginia*

OUR 8-year-old daughter had an emergency appendectomy. A few days later, I stopped at school where our son Justin was in kindergarten.

His teacher pulled me aside and asked about our daughter's surgery. She was confused because during show-and-tell, Justin had announced that his sister was "having her independence removed".
—*Susan LeBlanc Harrison, Arkansas*

I WAS about to leave after visiting my son and his family for the weekend and asked my 3-year-old grandson, Nathan, for hugs and kisses.

Little Nathan adamantly replied, "No kisses. You'll give me germs, and then I'll have to take a bath."
—*Jan Funk Hudson, Illinois*

MY daughter's neighbor was expecting her third child. When the time for the blessed event approached, my daughter asked the woman's 4-year-old, Devon, if she was going to help her mom deliver the new baby.

After thinking about this

Why was the broom late?
It over-swept.

for a few seconds, Devon replied, "Oh, no, we're going to keep the baby."

—Theresa Rogers
Elmhurst, Illinois

MY 3-year-old grandson, Mikie, had a runny nose, so I gave him a tissue. But first, I folded it into a triangular shape to make it easier for him to hold.

When I handed Mikie the tissue, he laughed and said, "Oh look, Grandma. You made a diaper for my nose." *—Evelyn Richter*
Center Point, Texas

A REAL YAWNER. "Denver was more than ready for bed," says Grandma Jane Pueschel, Sturgis, Michigan.

ON HEARING him say he had a "frog in his throat", my 4-year-old grandson shined a flashlight into his dad's mouth.

"I see him down there, Daddy," he exclaimed, "but I don't know how to get him out!" *—Edith Bowles*
Charmco, West Virginia

ABOUT A WEEK before I was expecting my second child, I thought it was time to explain to our firstborn, Joey, 4, a little bit about what to expect if I had to rush off to the hospital.

He started asking questions, and I explained that the baby was being cushioned by a large bag of water in my tummy.

He wrinkled up his nose, thought a bit and then asked, "Mom, won't that baby's jammies get all wet?"
—Cynthia Lambert
Boulder, Colorado

WHEN MY little brother Jimmy was 3, he discovered the big round vertebra at the base of his neck.

He asked our mother,

WISHFUL THINKING. "Jamie and Taylor look so intent as they blow the seeds from dandelions," says their mom, Teri Robinson, of Villa Park, California.

"What's that?" Not wanting to go into details, she answered, "That's part of what holds you together."

Jimmy's eyes grew big as saucers as he exclaimed, "You mean I can come apart?" —*Barbara Walker Fairfield, Illinois*

OUR daughter, 8, asked about the umbilical cords on our newborn puppies. I explained, saying they'd fall off in a few days.

Later that day, my mother stopped by, and my daughter was eager to show her the puppies.

"Look, Grandma," she exclaimed, turning one of the pups over for her to view. "They even have extension cords!" —*Beverly McKenzie Pulaski, New York*

MY 2-year-old grandson had a good way to describe his sore throat: "Mommy, my throat has a headache!" —*Helen Sharbono West Monroe, Louisiana*

SEVERAL DAYS after I had used some tape to patch a kitchen stool, my 3-year-old daughter asked, "Can I take the tape off? It should be all healed by now." —*Joyce Halvorson Albert Lea, Minnesota*

MY YOUNGEST son had just been to the doctor for a checkup. That evening as we were eating, I was pestered by a gnat and swatted it as it flew around me.

My 5-year-old daughter, who had come with us to the doctor, looked at me with a very serious expression on her face.

"Remember what the doctor said," she admonished. "There's a flu bug in the air." —*Linda Petersen McPherson, Kansas*

A FRIEND of mine developed laryngitis, much to the confusion of her 2-year-old son.

He climbed into her lap, pulled open her mouth and peered inside, saying, "What's wrong, Mommy? Did someone steal your batteries?" —*Marie Chapman Beech Grove, Indiana*

I OVERHEARD our 7-year-old grandson, Adam, quizzing his 3-year-old sister, Sarah, about the four seasons.

"Three of the seasons are spring, summer and fall. What's the other one?"

She promptly replied, "Flu season." —*Thelma Marshall Warren, Ohio*

The fourth commandment is not: Humor thy mother and father.

MILK MAID. "Our niece Leann was helping Grandpa milk the cow," says Kathy Dawson from Ewing, Michigan.

It's amazing what goes
through the minds
of little tots.

ANYBODY IN THERE? Kaitlyn Wheelock of Sioux Falls, South Dakota just had to have a peek inside a hollow log at nearby Newton Falls State Park.

AS OUR daughter's fourth birthday neared, she was taught to say she was "three and three-quarters" when asked how old she was.

One day her grandpa asked her age. She paused, obviously deep in thought, then burst out, "I'm three and three dimes!"

—*Carla Denham*
Chandler, Arizona

LITTLE Noah, our 3-year-old grandson, had just stubbed his toe. His brother tried to console him and asked which toe hurt. Noah answered, "The one that went to market."

—*Ruth Schiffer*
Allen Park, Michigan

ONE EVENING we were watching television when the power went out. From somewhere in the pitch blackness, daughter Beth, 3, piped up, "Hey, the house needs new batteries."

—*Hope Anderson*
Malta, Montana

I WAS helping my son Christopher brush his teeth when he started to talk. "Wait until I'm done brushing your teeth," I told him.

As I resumed brushing, he again tried to talk. In a firmer tone, I said, "Chris, wait until I'm done brushing your teeth."

When I finished brushing, I asked, "Now, what did you want to tell me?"

Chris replied, "That's not my toothbrush."
—Rebecca Cordova
Vancouver, Washington

OUR NIECE Staci and nephew James are thrilled when they spot deer. To encourage more of them to visit our yard, we decided to buy a salt lick.

When the storekeeper came out with the big block of salt to put it in the car, James' eyes got really big.

"Wow!" he exclaimed. "Too bad they don't make a sugar lick this big for kids."
—Linda Durst
Newman Lake, Washington

OUR AREA was experiencing a rash of severe summer storms, with the television news of death and destruction all around us.

When the tornado siren sounded one evening, I ran outside to help my 5-year-old son, Paul, bring in his toys.

As I closed the garage door, Paul turned for what he must have thought was one last look outside and said emphatically, "I'm sure going to miss myself."
—Shirley Oberle
Eau Claire, Wisconsin

ONE DAY when our family was driving on a bridge over a river, our 3-year-old daughter asked about an object floating in the water. We looked to see what she was referring to and told her it was a buoy.

When we crossed that river the next time, she got real excited and said, "There's that kid in the water!"
—Marilyn Ringel
Marquette Heights, Illinois

WE HELPED celebrate my 4-year-old nephew's birth-

If all the world's a stage, where does the audience sit?

day. He got a new tricycle, but it wasn't enough for him to simply jump on his new tricycle and pedal off.

Instead, he walked all around the trike, carefully looking it over. Squatting down, he peered underneath, then stood up and felt along the handlebars.

Finally, turning to his parents with obvious disappointment, he asked, "Where's the tape player?"
—*Nan Carol*
Atlanta, Georgia

WHEN OUR daughter was born, we already had three boys. They often heard people calling the new baby "precious" and "special".

One day, Sonny, who was 4, looked at his tiny sister and remarked, "Isn't she *preshul?*"
—*Norma Felsburg*
Gaylord, Kansas

I WAS dressing my 3-year-old son, Jason, for bed one evening, when he said, "Mommy, I like you."

I replied, "Well, I *love* you because you are my *son.*"

He then replied, "And you're my moon!"
—*Cindy Roach*
Dover, Pennsylvania

ONE hot summer day I gave my son, Danny, a Popsicle. It looked so cool and quenching, I asked him if I could have a lick.

He looked at me with surprise in his eyes, then shrugged his shoulders, came over...and licked my arm.   —*Dina Cohen*
Fort Lauderdale, Florida

OUR DAUGHTER Darla was using flash cards to quiz her boys, Davey, 7, and Jamie, 6, when this question came up: "What are the four seasons?"

Davey immediately answered, "Baseball, basketball, football and soccer!"

Darla asked him to try again and he replied, "Hunting, fishing, elk and antelope!" —*Marilyn Visser*
Langley, Washington

What's a frog's favorite flower?
Croak-us.

SHE'S GOT THE BLUES. "Our daughter Shanna had a good time at the blueberry patch," says Nancy Voak from Penn Yan, New York.

MY 22-month-old great granddaughter, Jessica, is being taught to say, "thank you" and "please".

Her grandparents recently took her to a restaurant. After they were seated, Jessica turned to everyone in the restaurant and said, "Thank you for coming."
   —*Helen Ferguson*
   Cedartown, Georgia

ONE AFTERNOON, it occurred to me that my 2-year-old daughter, Diana, had never seen me without a beard. So I decided to shave it off.

As I was finishing, I noticed Diana at the bathroom door with a shocked expression on her face. "Well, what do you think?" I asked.

She replied, gravely and urgently, "Dad, put it back on!"
   —*Jim Benefield*
   Escondido, California

WHILE HELPING his grandfather build a deck, our 5-year-old son, Kolin, hit his thumb with a hammer accidentally.

A couple of weeks later, his fingernail fell off. Kolin brought me the nail and asked, "Mommy, can I put this under my pillow for the fingernail fairy?"

—*Penny VanderFeen*
Hawarden, Iowa

KATIE, 2, and I usually sing songs just before bedtime. One night, she asked if we could sing the bunny song.

"I don't know any bunny songs," I said.

"Yes, you do," Katie insisted. "It is the one about the bunny sleeping over the ocean!"

Of course, she was referring to *My Bonnie Lies Over the Ocean.*

—*Paulanne Boettcher*
Esko, Minnesota

MY 5-year-old nephew, Sam, etched his name on the fender of his father's new truck with a rock. When his dad came home, he asked him why he had done such a thing.

"Didn't something in the back of your mind tell you that what you were doing was wrong?" his father asked.

Sam said, "I didn't hear anything, Daddy."

—*Joyce Montpelier*
Olla, Louisiana

ONE SUMMER, when my husband and 5-year-old son, Miles, were fixing fences at the ranch, Miles got to ride his own horse.

The horse was a slow walker and trailed far behind. When Miles finally caught up to his dad he said, "Dad, I don't like this horse…she won't obey my commandments!"

—*Venice Lancaster*
Afton, Wyoming

OUR YOUNG SON Don was the lucky winner of a baby duck that his second grade class had watched hatch. He named it "Jack".

I asked why he picked that name, and he quickly replied, "Mom, haven't you heard of 'Quacker Jack'?"

—*Mable Mortinson*
Cherokee, Iowa

WHILE I was reading with my 4-year-old son, he was telling me what he was seeing in the pictures. Being preoccupied with what I was reading, I apparently was not paying enough attention to him.

All of a sudden, he put his hand on my cheek and said, "Daddy, listen to me with your eyes." —*Mike Reber Harper, Kansas*

AFTER an hour of teaching our youngest tot, Roberta, the words to *Twinkle, Twinkle, Little Star,* our older children thought a solo performance was in order.

The words and melody flowed until Roberta forgot the line about "a diamond

in the sky". Quickly her big sister prompted her by pointing to the diamond ring on my finger.

Taking the cue, Roberta continued and sang, "Up upon the world so high, like a *knuckle* in the sky." —*Annabelle Farrell Lovington, Illinois*

MY NIECE'S 6-year-old daughter was visiting her grandma and grandpa when she was asked if she'd like something to eat.

"I sure would," she replied. "I'm so hungry my stomach is thundering." —*Donna Hibbard Walworth, Wisconsin*

MY HUSBAND, who is bald, was fixing a cupboard at a day care center, while a 3-year-old boy looked on. After watching my husband for a few minutes, the little boy asked, "Hey, do you know you don't have any hair?" —*Martha Hadley Sumner, Maine*

ROOTIN' TOOTIN' COWBOY. "Son yle loves to play cowboy," says Bev-ly Cessna, Cumberland, Md.

MY 4-year-old daughter, Haley, apparently had been

dreaming when I woke her up for breakfast. She looked at me with sleepy blue eyes and said, "Mommy, there was a movie in my eyes."

—*Nancy Hinrichs*
Goodhue, Minnesota

WHEN our veterinarian was 5 years old, her parents caught her sneaking bread from the dinner table to one of the family dogs.

Asked why she was feeding the dog, Karen answered, "You said if she gets bread, she'll have puppies, and I want some."

—*Paula Magnus*
Okanogan, Washington

BEFORE the birth of our daughter's second son, we were sitting around the dinner table one Sunday evening, discussing potential names for the new baby.

After listening quietly for a long time, our 5-year-old grandson, Callen, de-

EATING ON THE JOB. "Our daughter Jenna loves her pedal tractor...and she also loves chocolate, as you can see by her face," says Jennifer Rohret of Solon, Iowa

clared, "I don't care what all of you call him. I'm going to call him Stephen."

—*Ron Sinclair*
Riverside, California

I WAS teaching my 7-year-old daughter, Christin, a grammar lesson while 3-year-old Courtney was doing a puzzle.

During the course of the lesson, Christin got frustrated and yelled out, "I hate grammar!"

To our surprise, Courtney turned from her puzzle and said, "No, Christin, you *love* Grandma!"

Christin and I looked at each other and laughed about it the rest of the day.

—*Tami Smith*
Boys Ranch, Texas

MY NIECE Sara, 5, was listening to her parents discussing names for a soon-to-be-born baby. They decided on the name Allison for a girl, but were pondering over a middle name.

That's when Sara announced her suggestion: "Allison Wonderland".

Needless to say, new baby Allison Marie is often called "Allison Wonderland". —*Mary Ann Ochs*
Aberdeen, South Dakota

WE WERE at a wedding reception and in attendance were three pregnant women who were near the end of their terms.

During the evening, my 8-year-old daughter ran up to me, all excited, and said, "Mommy, Mommy, there are three ladies over there who are going to have babies."

"Shhh, Honey," I replied. "Not so loud."

She answered, "Why not, Mommy, don't they know it yet?" —*Martha Morris*
Fort Wayne, Indiana

GRANDMA gave my 10-year-old son a pogo stick for Christmas. He'd never seen one or heard of a pogo stick before, but he loved it.

One day he was playing

What do you say to a crying dog?
Hush puppy!

with it and said, "Mom it's something I wanted, and didn't even know I did."

—Phyllis Grupe
Stockton, California

ONE DAY while listening to my son, Michael, 4, talking to his friend, I had to chuckle when I heard him ask, "Your dad took you to work with him? Did he forget you were a kid?"

—Carol Allen
Auburn, California

JACOB, my 5-year-old grandson, dug a hole in the yard to look for earthworms. After he had his tin can full of worms, he filled the hole back in with soil.

Then he dug a second hole, dumped all his worms in and filled that hole back up, too. Asked what he was doing, Jacob answered, "When Daddy has time to take me fishing, I'll know where all the worms are."

—Penny Cooper
Adair, Iowa

THE NEEDLE on the compass on our car was pointing to "S". I asked my 5-

UDDERLY CONTENT. " 'Moo' was one of Mitchell's first words," says his mom, Pam Thompson, Osakis, Minn.

year-old daughter if she knew what that meant. She replied, "Yes, we're going *straight.*"

—Marilyn Hamilton
Kearsarge, New Hampshire

OUR DAUGHTER Brenda was stopped by a policeman for driving a little too fast. As the officer approached the car, Brenda's 3-year-old daughter, Katie, asked what was the matter.

"Mommy's in trouble," Brenda explained.

When the officer arrived, Katie promptly asked him

if he was going to give Mommy a spanking. He laughed so hard he ended up walking away without issuing a ticket!

—*Alma Braumley*
Grandview, Texas

THE naturally finished bunk beds, used by my brother and me when we were young, are now occupied by my daughters.

Laura, 6, asked what color the beds were when I was little. I told her that they were the very same color as they are now—brown.

She looked puzzled for a few moments, then replied, "But, Dad, everything back then was black and white!"

—*Wayne Clay*
Aberdeen, North Carolina

ONE early spring day, my 4-year-old son, Evan, said, "Mama, one of these days it'll be warm enough to wear short-sleeved pants."

—*Joan Heinle*
Eddyville, Iowa

MY HUSBAND and I took our 5- and 3-year-olds to see some Fourth of July fireworks.

When we came home that night, there was a quarter moon in the sky. My daughter looked up and asked, "Did the firecrackers break off a piece of the moon?"

—*Clemencia Ortega*
Yuma, Arizona

WITH THREE children, it seems as if we're always replacing worn-out batteries in toys.

One evening, daughter Kelley, who was 4 at the time, came to me holding a toy and two batteries. She looked up at me and asked, "Mommy, are these batteries really dead, or are they just sleeping?"

—*Mary Joan Jackson*
Manchester, Kentucky

WHEN our son Ryan was about 6, his grandparents took him fishing.

He had his own pole, but

What do frogs wear when they exercise?
Jumpsuits.

didn't know how to fish. Ryan's bobber suddenly went under the water, and his "maw-maw" exclaimed, "Pull on your pole, Ryan! Pull it in!" He did, and pulled in a nice catfish.

After Paw-Paw took the fish off and put the line back in the water, Ryan sat quietly for a few minutes, then said, "Tell me to pull it in again, Maw-Maw!"

—Martha Carr
Tallahassee, Florida

MY SISTER Thelma and her 4-year-old daughter, Donna, were in the car, singing songs to pass the time.

Thelma started singing, "Oh, my darlin', oh, my darlin'," and then Donna joined in, "Oh, my darlin', *lemon lime!*"

—Betty Myrick
Rushville, Indiana

OUR SON, Jacob, was visiting his grandparents shortly before his third birthday.

Grandpa was eating pistachio nuts and was explaining to Jacob what they were called.

When his grandmother asked him to say the word "pistachio", Jacob said, "I can't...my mouth's not big enough yet!"

—Holly Sperberg
Stevens Point, Wisconsin

ON A TRIP to visit my parents in Montana, we stayed overnight in a big hotel.

Our son, who was 3 at the time, looked out the window of our room on the 28th floor and saw a huge crane lit up with white lights.

Then he noticed a half moon in the sky and said, "Look, Mommy! They're fixing the moon!"

—Terry Elwess
Crestline, California

MY NEPHEW, Paul, who is 6, was talking with his grandfather about computers. When his grandfather mentioned that he didn't

Where do Eskimos practice for dogsled races? In mush-rooms.

have a computer, Paul replied, "But, Grandpa, how do you *think?*"
—*Patty Tschappat*
Illinois City, Illinois

MY YOUNG neighbors were surprised when they learned my cat had delivered a litter of kittens.

"Buffy had kittens?" one of the youngsters exclaimed. "We didn't even know she was married!"
—*Mrs. Byron Ebright*
Pasadena, California

AS I WAS sleeping on the sofa, my young daughter, Nancy, had gotten out of bed and come into the living room.

She woke me up by lifting one of my eyelids and asking, "Mommy, are you in there?" —*Dorothy Cohoon*
Kansas City, Missouri

MY NEPHEW Gordon was helping his 7-year-old son read a Christmas card from a relative.

Nicholas did quite well with the printed words, but he stopped when he got to the handwriting inside. Af-

LOVE AT FIRST SIGHT. "Jacie formed a close bond with 'Pinky' the pig," says her mom, Kim Lind, Hillsboro, Wis.

ter a long pause, his dad asked who had sent the card.

Exasperated, Nicholas replied, "I don't know, Dad. You know I can't read that fast writing yet!"
—*JoAn Ferguson*
McLean, Virginia

DURING ONE of our rare cold snaps here on the Gulf Coast, the radio had been forecasting freeze warnings all weekend, along with the wind-chill factor.

On Monday morning, our

first grader, Jamie, was putting on his sweatshirt and jacket as I told him it was 30° outside.

He said, "But, Mama, how cold is it at the windshield factory?"

—*Mrs. Raymond Davis*
Lucedale, Mississippi

 ONE DAY, years ago, my mother took my brother Bob to the grocery store. He was 4 at the time.

While she was paying for the groceries, the storeowner gave Bobby an apple. When he didn't say thank you, Mother prompted, "Bobby, now what do you say to the nice man?"

After thinking for a moment, Bobby replied, "Can you peel it?"

—*Vernon Blaziek*
Napa, California

WHILE our family was enjoying a show at our local civic arena, our son, 2, was intently watching a little girl eat some cotton candy.

After studying her for some time, he asked, "Mom,

why is that little girl eating fuzz?"
—*Kim Vince*
Dillonvale, Ohio

DAUGHTER Julie was watching the fireflies light up last summer. "Look!" she said. "They're putting on their brakes."

—*Paulette Graff*
Estherville, Iowa

I WAS in the car with my two boys when a bird flew right in front of us and I swerved. After a moment of silence, my son Dusty exclaimed, "That little bird didn't look both ways before he crossed the road."

—*Janeann Nelson*
Weirton, West Virginia

A NEW BABY had just arrived at 4-year-old Jami's house. When a neighbor inquired if it was a boy or a girl, Jami sighed and replied, "I don't know…they haven't dressed it yet."

—*Jolena Stockebrand*
Marshall, Arkansas

WHEN our daughter was born, I was constantly

NEIGH-SAYER. "Our grandson John Adams participated in a stick horse competition at a horse show," says Katie Myhan from Muscle Shoals, Alabama.

telling her she was the most beautiful girl in the world. When I fed her, changed her, anytime I was talking to her, I told her that.

One day when she was 4, Jeanne came into the back bedroom where I was cleaning and exclaimed, "Mommy, Mommy, that man is looking for me!"

"What man?" I asked.

"Come quick, he's looking for me," she said.

Fearing the worst, and

thinking that maybe there was a strange man in the house, I went running down the hall to the kitchen. Jeanne pointed to the radio and, sure enough, there he was, Charlie Rich, singing, *"Did you happen to see the most beautiful girl in the world…"*

Ah, the innocence of youth! —*Jean Jordan Canton, North Carolina*

I GET a good laugh every time I think of this episode when I was 9 months pregnant and *very* big. I was still working at the time, and my job required me to wear a pager.

While standing in line at the grocery store, my pager went off. The little boy behind me looked up at his mother and said, "Look out, Mommy, she's backing up."

I realize my pager sounds like a truck that's backing up, but I didn't think I was *that* big!
—*Polly Pearson Holdrege, Nebraska*

MY 4-year-old nephew, Jesse, was perched on a stool in his parents' egg room, watching his great-aunt help sort the eggs.

"How come you aren't married?" he asked her.

"Well, there just weren't enough men to go around," she replied.

Jesse regarded this thoughtfully for a moment. Then he said, "But it only takes one!" —*Donna Keener Turbotville, Pennsylvania*

WHEN my daughter Katrina was 3, she stood against the doorjamb and put her hand on top of her head.

She exclaimed, "See how much I growed…I'm all the way up to my hand!"
—*Shari Seymour Sutton, Vermont*

YEARS AGO, as I was hurriedly slathering on some facial cream, my daughter, who was 3 at the time, asked, "What is that for?"

To avoid a lengthy explanation, I answered, "To

What do you call a fancy dance at the North Pole? A snowball.

ROUGH RIDER. "After digging carrots, Karlee went for a 'ride'," says Grandpa Martin Zieser, Springville, Iowa.

you must be spoiled!"

"Oh, no," piped up one of the brothers, "she always smells that way."

—*Ann Taugher*
Monterey, California

WHEN our son Jaime was 4, his sisters were playing a word game in which one of the answers was "door".

To give Jaime a clue, they asked him what's the first thing he opens when he comes in the house.

"My mouth," he replied.

—*Jan Collado*
Thornton, Colorado

make me look pretty."

She looked up at me and said very seriously, "It isn't very good, is it?"

—*Zelma Dilks*
Holden, Missouri

A NEIGHBOR had four children—three boys and a girl, who was the youngest.

One day, an elderly relative from the Midwest came to visit. All of the children lined up to greet her, and when she came to the little girl, she said, "Well,

MY SISTER was trying to explain family relationships to her little granddaughter.

"Joanie is your aunt. Aunt Mary is your great-aunt and Aunt Frances is your great-great-aunt."

Little Jody thought for a while, then said, "Oh, I see. The older they get, the greater they get."

—*Mary Pendergraft*
Colton, California

MY DAUGHTER came in from swimming and told

SIZING THINGS UP. Spencer Anderson was looking at things from a different angle when Grandma Judy Kasl of Bothell, Washington snapped this photo.

me her cousin saw a "coat bee". I could not figure out what she was talking about.

When I asked my nephew about this, he laughed and said the "coat bee" was actually a yellow jacket.

—*Jacquie Offenbecher*
Massillon, Ohio

A REAL ESTATE client transferred to our area from Atlanta, Georgia.

As we walked up the steps of a particularly lovely home, I remarked, "The owner of the home says it doesn't have a flaw."

My client's 8-year-old son, who already had developed quite a Southern drawl, pulled on his mother's skirt and said, "Momma, if this house doesn't have a flaw, what are we going to walk on?"

—*Lawrence Timpe*
Chesterfield, Missouri

ONE DAY just before Christmas, I suggested to my 5-year-old daughter, Stephanie, that we turn on the stereo and listen to some Christmas music.

"Okay, but what else can we do?" she asked.

"What do you mean?" I responded.

"I need something to do with my hands," she replied. "Music only uses my ears!"
—*Jean Carver*
Jupiter, Florida

ON OUR first trip to Arizona, we took a sightseeing tour accompanied by our 9-year-old nephew who lives there.

After we "oohed" and "aahed" through miles of red mountains and wildflowers, he informed us quite seriously, "Now this is not spray painted. This is all natural!"
—*Sue Stacker*
Midland, Michigan

ONE rainy day, I took our twin daughters with me to the grocery store. The rain had caused the oil on the asphalt parking lot to run in many colors.

As we hurried across the lot to the store, one of the girls announced, "Look, Mom. The rainbow fell!"
—*Sue Drake*
De Funiak Springs, Florida

MY FRIEND was teaching her 4-year-old daughter about various denominations of coins. She laid five pennies on the table and explained, "Five pennies will make a nickel."

Just then the phone rang, and my friend went to answer it. When she returned, her little girl was staring at the pennies.

"When, Mommy?" she asked. "When will the five pennies make a nickel?"
—*Catherine Russo*
New Port Richey, Florida

WHEN my son, John, was very little, I asked him if he knew how many legs a cow has. He replied, "Two in the front, two in the back and two on each side."

He was correct, but somehow it didn't add up.
—*Laura Morse*
Candor, New York

What do you call a bunch of fighting fleas?
A flea-for-all.

BEST BUDDIES. "Steve and 'Smokey' were taking a break from playing", says Uncle Jerry Slovacek, San Diego, California.

City Kids and Country Cousins

Laughter abounds when
city children come callin'
in the country.

AFTER a trip to the doctor, my wife told our 4-year-old daughter, Caitlin, "We need to stop at the pharmacy to get you some medicine."

Caitlin replied, "Oh, good! I can't wait to see the cows and the pigs."

My wife was confused until she figured out that Caitlin thought she was talking about a "farmacy", not a drugstore.

—*Scott Quinn*
Schenectady, New York

MY FRIEND'S nephew, Derek, lives on a ranch. One day, when Derek was 3 years old, his dad pointed to an old windmill standing nearby and asked him if he knew what it was.

"Yup," Derek confidently replied. "That's a cow fan."

—*Jennifer Ferris*
Lexington, Texas

OUR 3-year-old grandson was visiting us from New Hampshire, where his father has a dairy farm.

One day we took him to the New England Aquarium, where he was fascinated by the penguins. After viewing all the other exhibits, we asked him if he was ready to go home.

Apparently he was getting a little homesick, because he replied that he wanted to see the penguins again since they looked like "little Holstein people".

—*Marjorie Erickson*
Weymouth, Massachusetts

WHEN our 4-year-old took his first trip to a farm, he was totally fascinated by the changes in scenery from city to country.

However, the trip back to town must have seemed arduous. When we finally left gravel roads behind and were driving on paved roads again, he perked up and asked, "Are we back in America now?"

—*Vincent Layton*
Cook Station, Missouri

AS I HELPED my husband harvest corn, our young daughter rode in the tractor cab with me.

While we were waiting in the field, three deer— two does and a buck— bounded out from some nearby trees. I explained to my daughter that deer without antlers are does and the ones with antlers are bucks.

A while later, the buck appeared again. Testing my daughter, I asked her what the deer with antlers is called. After thinking for a minute, she smiled and said, "A dollar!"

—*Diane Jacobson*
Galva, Iowa

MY GRANDSON Ed and his 4-year-old son, Matthew, came from New York City to visit me on a warm spring day. As we walked around the yard, I pointed out the dogwoods in bloom.

"With a puzzled look on his face, Matthew asked, "Will they get little doggies on them?"

—*Kathryn Adams*
Lititz, Pennsylvania

MANY winters ago, I went outside to get a chicken for dinner. My little daughter Rhonda wanted to go along.

Since it was very cold, I told her to stay inside, adding that I'd be back as soon as I dressed the chicken.

She responded, "But, Mama, I'd just *love* to see you put a dress on that chicken!" —*Glenna Parks*
Greenfield, Illinois

SQUEAL HAPPY. "Son Jeremy was thrilled to hold a 2-day-old runt," says Janelle Rackers, Jefferson City, Mo.

I'D TAKEN three of my grandchildren to a fair and stopped at the FFA petting barn. The kids were petting two heifer calves when the 5-year-old, Theresa, said, "Grandma, these are girl cows. Want to know how I know?"

A little hesitant, I asked

FOOD FOR THOUGHT. "I told our son Tim that he'd better watch out in case the hen thought his tongue was a worm," says Dave Barta, Goldendale, Wash.

her how she knew. "They have barrettes," she replied, pointing to the ear tags. "See?" —*Arlene Hecht*
Ionia, Michigan

RECENTLY, our 6-year-old grandson visited a farm. Afterward, he told us all about it. Some of the cows, he said, were older than his grandpa.

When we asked how he knew that, he responded, "They had tags in their ears with their ages on them, and one was 104."
—*Pam Jones*
Council Bluffs, Iowa

AT OUR county fair, a young boy was watching a sheep-shearing demonstration.

As the man completed the job, the impressed little guy asked, "Would you please undress another one?" —*Kathy Coleman*
Morton, Washington

MY parents had a farm back in the early 1930s. One day, our city friends dropped in for a visit.

My mom asked the kids if they'd like a glass of warm milk from our cow. The 6-year-old boy answered, "No, thank you. We don't drink milk from cows. We only drink milk from our milkman."

—*George DeCraemer*
Warren, Michigan

I OVERHEARD a conversation between my 6-year-old daughter, Danielle, and her best friend, Sarah, concerning horses.

"All I want is a cute little baby horse," Danielle said.

"If you want a baby horse, then you need to get your big horse bred," Sarah stated.

"Well," Danielle replied, "I'll feed her a whole loaf."

—*Tina Doucet*
Opelousas, Louisiana

WE WERE driving down a highway when our daughter, 3, noticed a salt block in the cattle pasture. She wanted to know what it was, so I told her it was salt for the cows.

She thought that over, then asked, "Where's their pepper?"   —*Vivian Lock*
Arkansas City, Kansas

OUR daughter, Lindsey, 4, is a very finicky eater. One night, no matter what I tried, I couldn't get her to eat anything, and I grew discouraged.

"What do you live on?" I finally blurted out.

Lindsey looked at me with wide, innocent eyes and said, "Why, a *farm*, Mommy."

—*Debbie Evenson*
Wahpeton, North Dakota

MY SISTER and her 3-year-old son, David, were visiting our farm, so I saddled our horses for a ride.

As I finished putting the bridle on "Hope", our little mare, I said to my sister, "You get on and warm her up before I put David up with you."

David touched the side of the horse and said, "She's already hot, Mom. Let's go!"

—*Kay Pittenger*
Wamego, Kansas

Why don't frogs park cars?
They're afraid they might get toad away.

rect part of his body.

"That's great, Mark. Now where's your calf?"

I waited for him to point to the lower part of his leg behind his shin, but after a moment's thought, he answered, "Down in the barn!" —*Teresa Stuecker Elizabethtown, Kentucky*

WE HOPE to own a farm someday, and my 8-year-old daughter is very excited whenever we talk about it. One day she came running in the door after school yelling, "I found the perfect farm. It has a big house, a big barn and lots of land."

I asked, "How do you know it's for sale?"

She replied, "Because there's a sign out front that says 'Hay for Sale'."
—*Lee Ann Crossman Vanderbilt, Michigan*

PICKIN' SOME FUN. "Our grandson Michael couldn't wait for the apples to ripen," says Joyce Buller, Dallas, Ore.

A FRIEND of mine was having a garage sale in town, so I gave her some brown eggs to sell.

A mother arrived with her little boy, who opened up my carton of eggs and exclaimed, "Look, Mom, chocolate eggs!"
—*Susan Shaferly Alvada, Ohio*

ONE DAY I was quizzing my nephew Mark, 3, on the general parts of the body—ears, elbow, knees and shoulder. Each time he quickly pointed to the cor-

WE WERE demonstrating a new alarm clock that crowed like a rooster to our grandsons Anthony and Bobby. After hearing it, Anthony asked, "How did a rooster get in there?"

Bobby quickly answered,

"It's too little for a whole rooster...they just put the beak in."
—*Roberta Rodriguez*
Dodge City, Kansas

ONE EVENING, I was talking about how big the mosquitoes were. My 6-year-old grandson piped up, "It's because they have more room to grow in the country."
—*Sharon Warmbrodt*
Snohomish, Washington

OUR GRANDSON Arthur went with his kindergarten class on a field trip to a dairy farm. Upon returning home that evening, he excitedly told his parents how everyone got to milk a cow.

"And how do you milk a cow?" his dad asked.

"Well, you sit on a stool beside the cow, and then you grab the gutters," Arthur replied.
—*Lloyd Stoops*
Sun City, Arizona

WE toured the Midwest in our motor home with our daughter and two young grandchildren.

While going through a small town in Iowa, we passed a commercial fertilizer plant.

"I wonder how they make fertilizer," I mused out loud. Jason, our 5-year-old grandson, immediately replied, "That's easy. Buy a cow and wait."
—*Mrs. Al Hiegel*
Conway, Arkansas

MY DAUGHTER Danielle and I were listening to Christmas songs on the radio while we 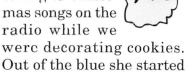 were decorating cookies. Out of the blue she started sobbing.

"Honey, what's wrong?" I asked.

"The radio said, 'Santa Claus is coming to town'," she answered. "But we live in the country!"
—*Darlene Buechel*
Chilton, Wisconsin

ONE MORNING, my son called and asked me to help him deliver a calf. When I arrived, he was in the barn with my two grandsons.

We got busy with the

cow. After the calf was born, one of the boys said, "If you had such a time getting him out, I don't see how you ever got him in there in the first place!"
—*Elmer Eberspacher*
Seward, Nebraska

WE WERE driving with our grandsons Cody, 3, and Jacob, 1, and passed a field where horses were grazing. Jacob, who thinks anything with four legs is a cow, pointed to them and said, "Cow."

Cody replied, "Those aren't cows. See, they're wearing horse faces."
—*Joan Williams*
Pueblo West, Colorado

MY DAUGHTER and two little granddaughters were visiting for a few days, taking a break from big-city living. One afternoon, I took them fishing.

As luck would have it, 4-year-old Haley caught the most fish, even though it was her first time fishing.

We had a stringer of eight good-sized fish, and she couldn't wait to call her dad.

When Haley's father asked her what she did with all the fish she caught, her immediate response was, "We put them on a leash." —*Doug Hopkins*
Eufaula, Oklahoma

ONE DAY our 6-year-old grandson, Joey, was over at our farm, spending time with his grandpa. He asked, "Grandpa, do you farm for money or fun?"
—*Sandra Dame*
Oldcastle, Ontario

ONE DAY as we were driving to church, my husband slowed down to let a big milk truck back into a farm driveway. Although we drive by dairy farms every day, our 4-year-old son, Brandon, had never seen cows being milked.

As he watched the truck backing up, Brandon asked, "Mom, does the milk

Why don't bats get sales calls?
Because they always hang up.

CUTE CANINES. Gertrude George's grandkids were having a ball checking out this litter of puppies, says Cindy Schmitt from Fairbanks, Alaska.

truck bring milk to the cows?" —*Edee McArtor Fairfield, Vermont*

AFTER returning home from seeing our neighbors' new hot tub, our son Levi, 3, asked, "When can we go back to see Ted's watering trough?" —*Karen Lustig Cottonwood, Idaho*

SOME friends of mine took their 5-year-old grandson to see a farm. When they came back, their grandson told me excitedly that he'd seen the farmer squeeze milk out of a cow.

He tried to tell the farmer that he was going to a lot of trouble. The little guy told the farmer, "At our house, we just take milk out of a bottle." —*Lee Treft Blackwell, Oklahoma*

OUR young grandson, who lives in the city, came to visit us at the farm.

After going for a walk with his grandpa, he came racing in the house to tell me, "Grandma, I saw a salad in your garden."

—*Sarah Sprowls Prosperity, Pennsylvania*

WHEN WE were on a vacation trip, our 3-year-old son, Nathan, saw his first Appaloosa horse. In his excitement he shouted, "Mommy, look! There's a dot-to-dot horse."

—*Sandy Moore*
La Verne, California

HERE CHICKEN, CHICKEN. "Bradley loves his chickens," says his mom, Susan Barrett, Poulsbo, Washington.

WE WERE going to our friends' farm and there was much talk among our three children about the animals there.

From the backseat came this question from 7-year-old Brian: "Mom, do you know what they call a baby goat?"

When I said I didn't know, he replied with confidence, "A children!"

—*Lisa Brown*
Marietta, Georgia

OUR 12-year-old daughter, April, wanted a dalmation for years, but we lived in town and had no room for such a large dog.

When we finally moved to the country, we went looking for a litter of dalmations. When we brought "Domino" home, April was thrilled, as was her 4-year-

old brother, Brent.

A few days later, Brent saw some Holsteins and suddenly yelled, "Hey, look! dalmation cows!"

—*Vicki Morrison*
Glasgow, Kentucky

ONE DAY I was driving down a country road in our neighborhood when we met a farmer in a pickup. My son Derek, 5, started jumping up and down, waving at the man excitedly.

Feeling a little embarrassed, I said, "Derek, you don't even know who that is, so why are you getting so excited?"

"Oh, yes, I do, Mom," he said. "That's Howdy."

A little perplexed, I asked more and he explained that earlier that week he'd been with Grandpa, and when they met that same truck Grandpa stuck his hand up to wave and said, "Howdy".

So Derek was sure he had the name right and that the farmer was a friend! —*Deb Earnhart Albion, Indiana*

MY SON Joey, 5, complained his new sneakers were too tight and hurt his feet, so we took them back to the shoe store.

The salesman gave us a bigger size and was about to throw the old ones in the garbage, because he said he couldn't resell them once they have been worn.

That's when Joey turned to me and said, "Mom, we can use them for parts!"
—*Rita Serafin Salinas, California*

OUR DAUGHTER'S 3-year-old city nephew, Alex, was visiting our farm and was fascinated with our herd of Angus cattle.

When the cattle went to the stock tank to drink, Alex watched in amazement. Finally, he turned to our daughter and asked, "Aunt Pat, why are the cows drinking from their bathtub?" —*Ellen Krueger Canton, Missouri*

ONE of our ostriches was having difficulty laying an egg. So my brother Steven, 3, said to the ostrich, "Why don't you just quit swallowing those big eggs?"
—*Laura Troyer West Farmington, Ohio*

MY AUNT took her two children to visit relatives in Georgia. Her son Austin was no more than 8 years old, and though raised in the country in Florida, he had never seen cotton growing before.

During the visit, my

Knock, knock. Who's there? Slater. Slater, who? Slater than you think!

aunt asked Austin to go pick a boll of cotton from a nearby field. He came back with both hands full of cotton.

"Mommy," he asked, "is this enough to fill a bowl?"

—*Gail Sherman*
Arlington, Texas

OUR SON, Carl, took his family to a farm near his house to pick pumpkins and look at the animals. There was a little pig the children could pet.

When Caitlyn, 5, felt the bristly hairs, she said, "That pig must use an awful lot of hair spray!"

—*Audrey Quist*
Helena, Montana

OUR children have obviously gotten used to our bartering methods.

A friend of ours offered to scrape our driveway. He couldn't finish the job in one day, so he parked his tractor in our pasture.

As he was leaving, our 6-year-old daughter offered

him one of her dogs. Our friend agreed and loaded the dog in his truck before heading home for the day.

Our 4-year-old son saw the tractor in the pasture and the dog riding in the back of our friend's truck. He looked at his sister and said, "Excellent trade!"

—*Lois Harris*
Mountville, South Carolina

MY granddaughter Aarrica had been living in the country for a year when her great-grandmother asked her if there were any steers on the farm.

Aarrica, who was 6, gave her a puzzled look and replied, "Of course. We've got an 'upsteers' and a 'downsteers'!"

—*Connie Boles*
Grand River, Iowa

SOME YEARS AGO, I was visiting my parents in the country. Jeff, my young nephew who also lives on a farm, was visiting, too.

We saw a stray kitten

Why did the cook think he was tough?
Because he could beat up an egg.

POP-EWE-LARITY. "Alisha McGinnis was thrilled the lambs liked her so much," says Grandma Sharin Arnot, Geraldine, Mont. "This was a moment she won't forget."

sitting on the back steps of the farmhouse. When Jeff and I went out to investigate, I said, "I wonder if it's a boy or a girl."

Jeff answered, "Just do what Daddy does—turn it over and look at the bottom of its feet!" —*Peggy Brewer Wytheville, Virginia*

AFTER moving from Vermont to southern California, our family was happy to be living next to a farm—it was like bringing a little of the ruralness of Vermont with us.

We'd been there only a short time when our neighbor added two black Angus bulls to his herd, and we talked about them at breakfast.

That afternoon, our 6-year-old daughter brought home a friend from school and proudly told her about the farm, concluding with: "And right over there are two black anxious bulls."

—*Faith Higley San Diego, California*

ONE AFTERNOON, my 5-year-old granddaughter, Becky, and her mother passed a field of wild mustard. When Becky commented on all the pretty yellow flowers, her mother explained that it was wild mustard.

A few days later, they

SEVERAL years ago, we were thinking about buying a dairy farm. Our daughter, who was 7 years old at the time, was eager to become a country girl.

She told us that her older brother could milk the cows and she could "egg" the chickens.

—*L. Leavenworth*
Clinton, Connecticut

WE PUT bright yellow ear tags in all our calves' right ears. When our 2-year-old niece came to look at the calves, she exclaimed, "Oh, they're so cute—they all have earrings on."

—*Dolores Shettel*
Malta, Montana

OUR 3-year-old daughter, Teresa, spent many happy hours one summer on the front porch of her great-grandmother's country home in Ohio eating sweet peas. Great-Grandma did not seem to mind shelling pea pod after pea pod for Teresa to enjoy.

When we returned to our city home, I took Teresa shopping with me. After I stacked several boxes of

BUNDLE OF JOY. "Emily is all smiles when holding a puppy," says Grandma Brenda Doney, Waynesboro, Pa.

passed a field of white flowers and Becky said, "Look, Mommy, a field of mayonnaise!"

—*Mina Royer*
Middleburg, Pennsylvania

ROBBIE, our 2-year-old grandson, was giving his city cousin a tour of our basement while I was retrieving canned vegetables from the shelf for supper.

When they came to the furnace room, I heard Robbie explain, "This is where Grandpa cooks his wood."

—*Mary Rauch, Newark, Ohio*

frozen peas in the grocery cart, her eyes grew big as she remarked, "Some grandma sure spent a long time shelling all those!"
—*Dorothy Saurer*
Kailua, Hawaii

OUR SON Kyle celebrated a birthday by having several friends sleep over, including one boy, Colin, who lives in the city.

We decided to let Colin gather eggs. He was very excited and couldn't wait to cook one for breakfast.

"I've never had home-made eggs before!" he said.
—*Anna Lizana*
Pass Christian, Mississippi

WE WERE driving across Kansas on vacation and our 5-year-old granddaughter, Jaclyn, was enjoying the sights, especially the beautiful fields of corn.

The wind was blowing hard and I remarked, "Looks like the wind could blow the corn down!"

Jaclyn replied, "Oh, no, it's planted deep, Grandma. And you don't blow down when you're planted deep."
—*Eva Moore*
Lebanon, Missouri

MY 8-year-old city grandson, Nick, and I were driving in our rural area when we came to a dairy farm. He said, "Look, Grandma, there's some cows. I don't get to see cows very often."

When I asked him what kind of cows those were, he replied with just a hint of doubt, "Two percent?"
—*Patricia Rylander*
Wyoming, Minnesota

OUR family was going through the small-animal barn at the county fair, looking at the many different rabbits.

Two little girls were strolling along, hand in hand, checking each cage. We then heard one remark to the other: "I wonder which one is the Easter bunny." —*Jan Lishan*
Vancouver, Washington

What did the beaver say to the tree?
It's been nice gnawing you.

GOOD COMPANY. "My father-in-law, Ray, sat with his goose, 'Roger', and grandson R.J.," says Jodie Butler, Edgewood, N.M.

It's no wonder grandparents
can't get enough of their
grandchildren.

AS I was nearing my 60th birthday, my daughters were teasing me about being an old lady. Of course, I reacted.

My 4-year-old granddaughter, Kellie Jo, came to my rescue with the perfect rebuttal.

"Grandma," she said, "don't think of being an older lady. Think of being an older kid."
—*Celia Gilmour*
Aptos, California

I WAS showing my 7-year-old granddaughter some pictures of me when I was her age. After studying them for several minutes, she proclaimed, "So everything was black and white back then." —*Joyce Joseph*
Tucson, Arizona

ON A Sunday afternoon, my granddaughter, Carrie, 5, offered to get the paper in for us, when her mother said, "Thanks anyway, Carrie, but there isn't any paper today."

Carrie replied, "Why? Didn't anything happen?"
—*Faye Latham*
Upper Sandusky, Ohio

AS MY grandson was trying to start his snowmobile, his two daughters, three nephews and two nieces were hovering around trying to get the first ride.

Finally, my grandson said, "The next one who says they want to be first will be the *last*."

His youngest daughter, 6, thought for a moment and said, "I want to be second!" —*Marge Srok*
Nevis, Minnesota

A WOMAN asked our darling granddaughter Jami how old she was.

"I'm 4," Jami said as she held up four fingers. "But I'll be 5 when my thumb comes up." —*Ann Everett*
Rogue River, Oregon

MY 3-year-old granddaughter, Amanda, and I

Why did the Eskimo leave work early?
He wanted to avoid mush-hour.

GRANPA'S GIRL. "After a trip to the rodeo, I caught my daughter Copelin and her Grandpa Dean taking an ice cream break," says Tammy Pauly, Bonita Springs, Fla.

were watching a mother bird feed her baby. When the mother flew away for more food, another bird landed close to the baby. That's when Amanda observed, "That must be the baby-sitter."

—*Mrs. George Fultz*
La Porte, Indiana

OUR 5-year-old grandson, Ryan, was riding with his father when they spotted an old bleached turtle shell. "Please stop the truck, Dad. I want that turtle," he said.

His dad explained that there was no longer a turtle

inside the shell. After thinking about it for a minute, Ryan then asked, "Do you mean there's a naked turtle walking around here somewhere?"

—*Lucille Payne*
Cross Plains, Texas

MY SISTER was staying at the home of her daughter and 10-year-old grandson. While there, she got a glimpse of herself in a mirror and shrieked, "Oh, I look so awful."

Her grandson, who was by my sister's side, tried to comfort her. "You look okay,

FAST FRIENDS. "My father, Russel Spiess, and his great-grandson Cosbie Hollenbeck became buddies right after meeting," says Wanda Hollenbeck, Lancaster, Calif.

Grandma," he said. "It's an old mirror." —*Jan Unsicker Fountain Valley, California*

MY 5-YEAR-OLD grandson was studying reptiles in kindergarten and was intrigued with pythons. I told him pythons like people, so they hug them.

He responded, "Yeah, but they give mean hugs."
—*William Tonks Concord, New Hampshire*

WHILE baby-sitting our 5-year-old granddaughter, Jammie, I was refinishing a chest of drawers for our older granddaughter Jennifer. I got some sandpaper and was heading for the back porch, when Jammie asked where I was going.

When I told her I was going out to sand Jennifer's chest, Jammie came running with some sandpaper, too, saying, "Wait up, Grandma. I'll sand her neck!" —*Betty Rickles Cheyenne, Wyoming*

WHEN my great-granddaughter Bethany was about 4 years old, she looked at me with a puzzled expression and asked, "Why do you have white hair?"

I answered, "Because I am getting old."

She thought about this, then replied, "Well, I'm not going to get old. I'm going to stay new."

—*Inez McKinnon*
Bokchito, Oklahoma

I'D MADE myself a gingham dress and had enough fabric left over to make a matching dress for my granddaughter Elissa. Later, we wore our matching dresses to a birthday party. I sat down and put Elissa on my lap. But she quickly got off.

"Grandma, we'd better not be too close together," she said. "We'd look like one big lady with four legs!"

—*Barb Kinkaid*
Hartington, Nebraska

OUR grandson drew a picture of a boy and gave it to me. After much praise, I said, "But you forgot to put ears on the little boy."

He looked at the picture and said, "He doesn't need ears. No one is talking to him."

—*Bonnie Tryon*
San Luis Obispo, California

IT WAS a nice fall day when a friend brought my grown daughter a bouquet of cattails. They were lying on the counter when my 4-year-old grandson, Shaun, spied them.

"What are those?" he asked his mother.

When she told him, he eyed the cattails thoughtfully for a while, then asked, "How do you get them off the cat?"

—*Mrs. Park Cowles*
West Union, Iowa

WHILE VISITING us at our mountain home in Arkansas, our granddaughter tried to imitate the calls of birds she heard each evening.

We kept hearing one particular bird, but could never see it. Our granddaughter continued to return its call, until one night she asked, "What's it going to

---

Where do ghosts buy stamps?
At the ghost office.

do when it finds out I'm not a bird?" —*Inez Conner Riverview, Florida*

said, "Yeah, let it go. I don't want to give it a bath either." —*Elaine English Ashland, Illinois*

OUR son-in-law is an Air Force chaplain. When he was transferred to a new base, he and his family had their choice of two empty houses.

After inspecting the first one, 4-year-old Heather announced that she didn't like it. And after looking at the second house, she said the same thing.

"Just what don't you like about them?" her puzzled parents asked.

"They don't have any beds!" she replied.

—*Mrs. F.N. Arnold Falls City, Nebraska*

WHILE I was on vacation, my 5-year-old granddaughter, Ashley, came to stay with me at our cabin.

We went fishing and caught a catfish. After another hour, we decided to stop, so I told her we'd release the catfish because I didn't feel like cleaning it.

She pulled the fish basket out of the water, looked at it for a few seconds and

MY 5-year-old grandson was gazing intently at his great-grandmother one day. At last he asked, "Granny, are you a lot older than my mother?"

Granny smiled and told him, "Yes, dear. I'm a *lot* older than your mother."

My grandson nodded his head. "I thought so," he said with satisfaction. "My mom's skin sure fits a lot

WINGED WONDER. "Her Great-Aunt Marlies showed my niece Holly a pigeon," says Chris Talbot, Burke, Va.

better than yours does."
—*Mrs. A. W. Andrews*
Madison Heights, Virginia

To which he replied, "Gosh, Grandma, can deer read?" —*Meriam Bolinger*
Frankfort, Indiana

GRANDSON Josh came to spend a week. One afternoon we had company over, and my friends asked Josh how many more days he'd be staying.

"Just a minute," he called over his shoulder as he ran to his room. "I'll go count my underwear."
—*Mrs. C. Kebler*
North Java, New York

OUR 4-year-old grandson called me on the telephone all excited about the fish he had caught.

"We gave it to a friend. He is going to peel it for us," he said. —*Sharon Wood*
Maddock, North Dakota

MY GRANDSON, a freckled 5-year-old, and I were driving along when we watched several deer coming across a field, fleeing hunters in a nearby wooded area.

I said, "They're okay now on this side of the road. See the 'No Hunting' sign?"

WE took our 3-year-old grandson to the airport to  watch the planes take off.

After a big jet lifted off right near where we were parked, then made a big turn and passed back over us, high above, Casey asked, "Grammie, how come planes shrink when they get up in the air?"
—*Patricia Buck*
South Casco, Maine

WHILE watching me remove the ashes from our fireplace, my little granddaughter inquired, "Mammaw, is that melted wood?"
—*Jackie Riffle*
Iron Station, North Carolina

MY 3-year-old granddaughter was helping me remove leaves from the window wells. It was rather crowded down there, so I said, "Close quarters, Jenny."

When we moved to the

next window, Jenny was quick to point out, "Close pennies, Grandma."

—Eleanor Norberg
Downers Grove, Illinois

OUR 4-year-old granddaughter, Nicky, was elated when she got a bunny rabbit for her birthday.

Her granddad teased her by asking, "I wonder if he'd make great soup."

"Grandpa," Nicky exclaimed, "you know rabbits don't know how to cook!"

—Helen Dietrich
Bismarck, North Dakota

WHILE visiting our son and his family, we noticed that our granddaughters Macee and Mandee liked to eat sunflower seeds in the shells. When we went shopping, I bought a bag of shelled sunflower seeds.

I explained to the girls that these were just like the kind they had eaten before, only that the shells had been removed.

Mandee objected, "I can't eat these, Grandma. Someone else had them in their mouth." *—Sarah Stutzman*
Fort Wayne, Indiana

ATTENDING his first wedding, my grandson asked why brides wear white.

When told white represents happiness and innocence, he thought for a moment, then asked, "Why does the groom wear black?" *—Dick Schimmel*
Milwaukee, Wisconsin

MY 7-year-old grandson was riding with his mother, who was reciting tongue twisters.

After unsuccessfully trying to repeat them, he finally said, "You have to remember that my tongue is young." *—Ruby Covington*
Cross Plains, Tennessee

OUR GRANDSON Devin, 7, received a fortune cookie that said, "You are the kind of person who will go places."

What do Eskimos use to hold their houses together? Ig-gloo.

LOOK-ALIKES. "I had a good chuckle when I saw my son Brandon and my dad, Bob, striking the same pose," says Krista Nowalk from Greene, New York.

After thinking about this for a moment, he exclaimed, "Yeah, that fits me—I've been to Disneyland, I've been camping and I'm going to Black Butte!" —*Ray Ruckert Albany, Oregon*

MY 3-year-old grandson was standing at the edge of a large, shallow puddle of water pretending he was fishing. He was warned by his mom not to get his feet wet, but, you guessed it, a short time later Matthew was muddy up to his knees.

When asked why he disobeyed, he replied, "Mom, a fish pulled me in." —*Elizabeth Bergren Whitman, Massachusetts*

MY HUSBAND was washing the car when our 3-year-old granddaughter came and asked if she could help. He told her she could wash the whitewalls.

A little while later, he looked over and she was washing the side of the house. My husband asked,

"What are you doing?"

She replied promptly, "I'm washing the white walls." *—Marilyn Ringel Marquette Heights, Illinois*

MY 3-year-old grandson gave me a big hug and kiss and said, "Oh, Grandma, I love you."

Since he's a bit partial to me, I said, "Now go tell Grandpa that; he likes to hear it, too."

So he ran over to his grandfather, put his arms around him and said, "Oh, Grandpa, I love your wife." *—Leona Swisher Mulkeytown, Illinois*

OUR 4-year-old grandson was admiring our couch, which has an afghan over the back. "Grandma," he said, "we've got a couch at home just like that...but it doesn't have a sweater like yours." *—Lois Miles Darien, Illinois*

OUR granddaughter Melinda was excitedly telling me about the new kitten she just got.

"What color is your kitty?" I asked.

"White," she replied.

"Does it have spots?" I inquired.

"No," she said, "but it has fleas." *—Kaye Bradford Hudson, North Carolina*

A BIG HELP. "Son Austin got some help walking from Great-Grandpa Thomas," says Lana Smith, Enoch, Utah.

I WAS driving one day with my granddaughters in the car. As I was getting ready to make a turn, I announced, "Oh, I turned my signal on to turn right when I meant to go left."

Little 5-year-old Teresa

said, "Grandma, I learned my right from my left in nursery school."

—*Mrs. Charles Hall*
Tampa, Florida

MY 5-year-old granddaughter, Emily, wanted me to play a new card game with her. I told her she would have to teach me the rules.

Emily looked at the back of the card box and pretended to read, "Grandmas lose and kids win."

—*Lois Magee*
Seabrook, Texas

OUR GRANDDAUGHTER Jessica asked her mom what Grandpa did for a living. Her mother said, "Grandpa doesn't work anymore. He's retired."

A few days later when we were all together, Jessica said to her twin sister, Christine, "You know that Grandpa doesn't work anymore. He's really tired."

—*Lorraine Blank*
Madison, Wisconsin

DURING a recent visit, our 3-year-old granddaughter, Rachel, put on her roller skates and told us, "I'm learning to skate."

Just then, she stumbled a bit, and I caught her before she hit the ground. "I'm also learning how to fall," she said.

—*Jane Merritt*
Bloomingburg, Ohio

MY 3-year-old grandson, John, loves to listen to music, and I often play old-time Appalachian songs for him.

One day while John was drawing, his dad noticed he was coloring the grass blue and suggested he make the grass green instead.

To which John replied, "No, Daddy, Grandma loves bluegrass."

—*Patricia Larsen*
Hayesville, North Carolina

WHEN our 3-year-old granddaughter, Erica, told us she wanted to grow bigger, we asked her how big

Knock, knock. Who's there? Boo. Boo, who?
Why are you crying?

FUNNY BUNNY. "I laughed when I saw my grandsons Andrew and Axel intently studying this decorative rabbit," says Pat Ott from Conway, Arkansas.

she wished to be.

"Big enough to turn on the light switch and open the freezer door," Erica replied. —*Donna Toney Greenfield, Indiana*

HOLLY, my 2-year-old granddaughter, had been sent to "time out" on several occasions at preschool.

One day, Holly's mom had a number of errands to run and was in a hurry when she picked her up from preschool. Holly was being quite pokey and her mother scolded her about needing to move faster as she buckled her in the car seat.

Holly responded by cupping her little hands around her mother's face, and with much concern, she said, "Mommy, do we need time out this afternoon?"

—*Carol Zimmerman McGregor, Texas*

MY 6-year-old grandson recently asked his mother if he could drive their car. His mother explained that he's too young now, but someday he could.

Curiously, his mother

asked, "What makes you think you can drive a car?"

He replied, "Because the sign in front of my school says, 'Children Drive Slow'." —*Duane Hammond Milford, New Hampshire*

WE JUST LOVE having our 4-year-old grandson, Joshua, sleep over. Following breakfast one morning, I told him I was going to wash my face and get changed.

Hearing that, Joshua responded, "Oh, Grandma, don't change your face. I love it." —*Judy Piana Little Falls, New York*

WHEN granddaughter Dara was 3 years old, she was looking through our wedding album. Suddenly, she looked up at me and asked, "Grandma, is this when you and Grandpa were *new*?"

—*Patricia Bonetti Fairfield, Connecticut*

OUR grandson Tommy, 4, was spending the night with us. I had just tucked him in after reading *The*

Three Little Pigs when a thunderstorm came up.

"Grandma, I want to go home," he cried.

"Why?" I asked him. "You're safe here."

"No, I'm not," he replied. "My house is made of brick—yours is only made of wood."

—*Madeline Robinson Mountain Home, Arkansas*

OUR daughter specializes in making fall flower bouquets for her home.

One morning she asked her 4-year-old son if he'd like to go out in the country with her to cut cattails along the road in ditches to make her fall arrangements pretty.

The 4-year-old was very quiet during the ride. Finally he spoke up, with a tear in his eye, to ask, "Mom, after you cut the cattails, can I keep the cats?"

—*Lorraine Clark Mitchell, South Dakota*

MY HUSBAND and I recently hung an old painting

of George Washington in our living room. We figured when our two young grandsons came to visit again, the painting could be used to give them a little history lesson.

But when he saw the picture, 5-year-old Chris said, "Look! There's the dollar bill man!" —*Joyce Vaughan*
Cassville, Missouri

ONE winter evening, after attending a local basketball game, my grandson slipped slightly on some ice as he carried his 2-year-old daughter out of the gymnasium.

She quickly piped up, "Daddy, if you're going to fall, please put me down first!" —*Mathilda, McClure*
Lake Park, Iowa

WE LIVE in the woods of northern Minnesota. When our 8-year-old granddaughter was visiting one summer, I told her that bats are very beneficial. "They eat mosquitoes," I explained.

"The bats must be fasting tonight," she grumbled, swatting a mosquito off her arm. —*Kathy Miller*
Aitkin, Minnesota

IT WAS starting to get dark while I was out walking with my 3-year-old grandson, Brandon.

Suddenly he looked up at the sky and said, "Hey, Grandma! We'd better get home. They're turning off the sky!" —*Betty Wickewire*
Lehigh, Iowa

DURING a telephone conversation with our 4-year-old granddaughter, I was trying to explain why I couldn't come over and play with her.

Unable to grasp that 2,000 miles separated us, she asked in exasperation, "Grandma, where do you live?"

I told her that her grandfather and I lived in the woods in the state of Washington. She had to think

---

What do you use to clean a tuba?
Tuba-paste.

EVERY LAST DROP. "Getting all the juice from the watermelon wasn't a problem for granddaughter Cherianne and my husband," says Mary Harvath, Punxsutawney, Pa.

about that for a few seconds.

"Oh! I thought you lived in a house!" was her startled reply. That explained everything!

—Marian Yunghans
Bellingham, Washington

OUR children and grandchildren were over for Sunday dinner when the doorbell rang.

One of the granddaughters, Morgan, who was 4, went to the door to see who it was. "Is it the paperboy?" her mother asked.

Morgan, with all her wisdom, replied, "No, Mommy,

it's a *real* boy!"

—Bill and Sharon Burnridge
Simi Valley, California

MY 8-year-old granddaughter got up one morning with her hair flying every which way, full of static electricity.

When she looked in the mirror, she cried, "Grandma! While I was sleeping, someone came in and electrocuted my hair!"

—Gerry LeBlanc
Canton, Maine

OUR 6-year-old granddaughter, Kelly, is a great

SOLE SEARCHING. "Future ropers have to start somewhere, so why not on Grandpa's foot?" says Patti Wanke of Seabeck, Washington. "Ethan was so proud of himself."

communicator. If she isn't talking to a person, she's talking to her kitten, a doll, clouds, bees—whatever's around.

One day I asked her very cautiously, "Do you ever get into trouble at school for talking too much?"

Her reply was prompt and concise: "Grandma, I know when to keep my mouth quiet—but my brain is *never* quiet!"

—*Betty Ziska*
Ravenna, Ohio

I ASKED Katie, my 3-year-old granddaughter, to come with me to visit a shut-in friend. While there, my friend asked Katie if she got her pretty brown eyes from her mom or her dad.

Katie put her hands on her hips and without any hesitation replied, "They came with my body!"
—*Thelma White*
Sand Lake, Michigan

WHILE visiting us, one of our little granddaughters was having trouble going to sleep one night.

I sat on her bed in the dark and asked what was wrong. She got a little tongue-tied trying to tell me. Finally she blurted out, "Grandma, turn on the light so I can see to talk."
—*Irene Martin*
Birch Tree, Missouri

WHILE STAYING at my daughter's, I slept in the same room as my granddaughter Kristen, 3. In the morning, I woke up to find Kristen staring at me—her face about 3 inches from mine.

Gingerly, she touched my hairnet and asked, "Gram, did spiders do this to your hair while you were sleeping?"
—*Pat Miessner*
Mancelona, Michigan

DURING A DRIVE to town on a road undergoing major reconstruction, our 4-year-old grandson, Justin, was very caught up in the activity of the workers and the heavy equipment.

"I want to do that someday, Grammy," he said.

His interest was just as strong on the return trip. "I sure hope they don't get done before I grow up!" he remarked. —*Louise Harter*
Springport, Indiana

DURING a visit with my 8-year-old grandson, while I was looking for something I'd misplaced, I muttered, "I think I'm losing my marbles."

My grandson shot back, "When you find them, Grandma, can I play with them?" —*Mary Jones*
Twentynine Palms, California

What kind of dog can tell time?
A watchdog.

APPLE OF HER EYE. "Expressive Hannah Flowers was happy to pick apples," says friend Larry McGraw, Kimberly, Oregon.

Homegrown Humor

These great gardening tales
will guarantee some giggles.

A SWEET BEET. "Granddaughter Leah picked this huge sugar beet at our farm," says Bernice Hall, Edinburg, N.D.

OUR little granddaughter Stephanie was helping my husband water the garden. He asked, "Do you know whose garden this is?"

She replied, "It's Gram's garden."

Later, when they were watering the flowers, he queried, "Do you know whose roses these are?"

Stephanie answered, "They're Gram's roses."

Still later, they were working around the wishing well, and he asked, "Do you know whose wishing well this is?"

She said, "It's Gram's wishing well."

He replied, "Well, if Gram has the garden, roses and wishing well, what do I have?"

She looked up, smiled and said, "You have Gram!"
—*Vivian Dick*
Mill Hall, Pennsylvania

FOR SEVERAL YEARS, our grandson Sam and I have planted sapling trees around our farm.

One spring, I also planted sweet peas in a flower bed and stuck a dead branch in the ground to support the vines. Our summer was too hot and dry, so the peas never grew.

That fall as Sam and I walked past the flower bed, he remarked in a very serious tone, "Grandma, I don't think that branch is going to grow."
—*Betty Ziska*
Ravenna, Ohio

MY HUSBAND and I decided to put a rock garden in an area where grass wouldn't grow. Matt, a little neighbor boy, came over to watch while I set the smaller rocks in place.

He asked what I was doing, so I told him about my plans for a rock garden as I continued working. When I had finished the job, I watered the area to clean off the rocks and settle the soil around them.

Apparently, this was too much for Matt, because he finally said, "Don't you know that no matter how much you water those rocks, they aren't ever going to grow?"

—*Lois Perrine*
Canova, South Dakota

OUR FAMILY was picking apples one fall day when our son picked up a half-rotten apple from the ground.

"Look, Mom," he said. "This one already has cinnamon on it!"

—*Donna Goodson*
Jackson, Missouri

OUR 4-year-old son was watching his grandma dig potatoes from her garden.

"Those potatoes look good, Grandma," he said.

"Where's the gravy plant?"

—*Wint Johnsrud*
Portland, Oregon

ONE YEAR we planted white eggplant instead of the usual purple variety in our vegetable garden. One day my 5-year-old niece, Crystal, was with me in the garden and started to examine the white oval vegetable.

"What plant is this?" she asked. I told her it was an eggplant.

"Oh, my," she exclaimed. "I'm going right home and tell Mama about this. She's been buying eggs at the grocery store."

—*Phyllis James*
Franklin County, Virginia

I WAS SHOPPING for bedding plants at our local nursery with my 4-year-old grandson, David. After about an hour of looking at flowers, David took my hand and asked, "Grandma, can we go somewhere else? This place doesn't

The sooner you fall behind, the more time you'll have to catch up.

even have any dandelions."
—*Anne Marie Dancer*
Clare, Michigan

EMILY, my 2-year-old great-granddaughter, was following her grandmother, "Nana", around the garden. Later, she explained to me and her mother that she and Nana were growing green beans, corn and chickens.

When we questioned her about growing chickens in the garden, Emily marched us outside and pointed to the eggplant.
—*Marian Sue Birge*
Lebanon, Indiana

ONE SPRING DAY when we were having sesame seed rolls with our dinner, my daughter began piling up the sesame seeds that fell off the rolls.

When the meal was over, she asked, "Mommy, if we plant these seeds, will bread grow?"
—*Evelyn Anderson*
Aurora, Colorado

OUR 3-year-old granddaughter, Heather, was watching me prepare the garden to plant squash. As I dug a hole and dropped some seeds in it, she asked, "Will those seeds grow into squash?"

When I assured her they would, she ran across the yard, scooped up our pet cat and hurried back.

"Quick, Grandma, dig another hole," Heather pleaded. "I want to grow some kittens."
—*Pearl Betzko*
Ulster, Pennsylvania

A COUPLE of summers ago, my son Nicholas was outside playing when he brought a big cucumber to his grandpa. Nicholas was 2 at the time and so little that he had to use both arms to hold the cucumber.

When Grandpa Ken asked Nicholas how he grew such a big cucumber, Nicholas answered, "With Miracle Whip, Grandpa."

Grandpa Ken just about fell over laughing. He knew

What do monsters wear on their feet in winter? Ghoul-ashes.

HE CAN DIG IT. "Our son Elijah had all he could handle when we dug up these giant potatoes," says Lisa Barth-Main from Central City, Iowa.

Nicholas had seen him on many occasions fertilizing his garden with Miracle Gro. —*Jill Weaver*
Phoenix, Arizona

OUR granddaughter Kersten helped my husband plant a small patch of okra. Each afternoon, we'd check if the plants had sprouted.

Eventually, some sprouts started showing, and Kersten was so excited. "Grandpa, your fried okra is coming up," she reported. —*Sheila Morrison*
McKinney, Texas

SEVERAL WEEKS after planting a garden, my 5-year-old granddaughter, Renee, wanted to help her mother with yard work.

She went outside and returned later, saying she

BUCKETS OF FUN. Nathan Janowski kept an eye on his brother Peter as he picked peas in the family garden near Greer, South Carolina.

had pulled weeds in the garden.

"How did you know what plants were weeds?" her mother cautiously asked.

"Oh, that was easy, Mommy," Renee replied. "The picture on the seed package shows that tomatoes are red, so I just picked everything that was green."

—*Harriet Robinson*
Vacaville, California

MY great-nephew, 3, had lined up shelled corn on the living room carpet. His mother saw it and told him to clean it up.

"But, Mom," he replied, "I just planted it. I'll harvest it in a couple of months."

Needless to say, it was a short growing season.

—*Mary Knight*
New Athens, Ohio

I PLANTED two new flower beds and spread some pine bark chunks for ground cover. Since the flowers were new, I also applied fertilizer.

After a while, I replaced the small pine bark chunks with larger chunks, hoping they would provide better cover. Later that afternoon my youngest daughter came running excitedly into the house.

Having noticed my improvements, she breathlessly told me, "Wow, that new fertilizer really must work. It made the bark chunks grow *huge!*"

—*Roxann Brown*
West Fork, Arkansas

MY HUSBAND worked one spring day to prepare a plot of ground for a garden.

That night at the dinner table, he told our son and daughter that they could each have a row of their own to plant.

Son Greg said he wanted to plant watermelons, strawberries and beans. When daughter Beth was asked what she wanted to plant, she firmly replied, "Pork chops!"

—*Cheryl Jones*
Talbott, Tennessee

ONE SPRING, 5-year-old Bridgette had helped plant the flower bed by opening the seed packages for her mother. Soon afterward, she visited her grandparents' ranch in Montana.

Upon being told that the huge fields of wheat were all Grandpa's, she sighed sympathetically and said, "Poor Grandpa. He had to open *all* those packages of seeds!"

—*Venus Bardanouve*
Harlem, Montana

OUR granddaughters Tamara, 6, and Kasey, 4, spotted a  bird's nest in their yard one spring day. The nest contained four little blue eggs, and the girls watched daily as the babies began to emerge.

When the last one finally hatched, Kasey peered into the nest and excitedly announced, "They all bloomed!"

—*Judith Mayrwieser*
Wilmore, Kentucky

OUR 5-year-old daughter, Mesa, decided she wanted to plant peas and carrots in the garden. Her younger sister Molly asked her what peas are.

"Those are the little

round green things that come in their own sleeping bags," she explained.

—*Ty Covill*
River Falls, Wisconsin

A FRIEND of mine asked her 3-year-old son, Matthew, to pick some tomatoes from their vegetable garden. She emphasized that he should only pick the red ones.

He promptly replied, "I got it, Mom—pick the Internationals, leave the John Deeres."

—*Virginia Miller*
Elizabeth, Indiana

SPENDING a week at Grandma and Grandpa's farm was very special to our daughter Elizabeth, 3. She was helping them prepare green beans for canning and asked why they had so many.

They told her it was so they could have beans to eat during the winter months.

Elizabeth looked at the beans and said, "I'm not going to be *that* hungry!"

—*Sharon Peterson*
Lincoln, Nebraska

OUR 4-year-old granddaughter stumped me with a simple question. She came inside with a ladybug on her finger and a serious look on her face.

"Grandma," she asked, "what are *daddy* ladybugs called?"

After 48 years of living in the country, I had to admit I didn't have an answer for that one!" —*Donna Langolf*
Perryton, Texas

MY 2-year-old granddaughter, Nicole, was helping her mother decide what they should plant in their new garden.

"Mommy," she said very seriously, "I want to plant some macaroni and cheese." —*Dolores Wagner*
St. Louisville, Ohio

MY 3-year-old grand-

Why do dinosaurs laugh easily?
They have very big funny bones.

SEEDS OF THE FUTURE. Delbert Schlabach got a helping hand from his daughter Judith while planting the garden, says his wife, Susan, of Nappanee, Indiana.

daughter ran into our kitchen and said, "Granny, I want to see the biscuits."

"Well we're not having any biscuits for breakfast," I replied.

"No, I mean I want to see the biscuit bush," she insisted, pointing out the window to the blooming red hibiscus bush.

—*Marilyn Kayton*
Naperville, Illinois

WHEN our son Galen was 5, we took him to a farm to pick out a pumpkin to carve for Halloween.

As we walked around, he spotted dozens of green crookneck squash for sale, all stacked against each other.

"Oh, man," Galen exclaimed. "These people sure know how to grow big green beans!"

—*Deborah Brothers*
Springfield, Illinois

WITH the first signs of spring in western Tennessee, my niece Cynthia took her 3-year-old daughter, Jenny, to pick a bouquet of forsythia.

As the little girl carried them, she was told, "These are forsythia."

"No, no," came the quick response from Jenny. "These aren't for Cynthia—they're mine!"

—*Patricia Muncy*
Bland, Virginia

ONE of my twin grand-daughters, Rebekah, came in the house with a flower for her mother. When my daughter asked Rebekah where her sister, Hannah, was, she replied, "Oh, she's still out-side waiting for her flower to bloom." —*Ruth Davis*
Live Oak, Florida

MY 6-year-old grandson had been keeping an eye on a robin's nest. When the eggs hatched, he asked what happened to the eggshells.

His mother said, "Maybe the mother bird put them out in the garden like I do."

After thinking a minute, he said, "Is *that* how we get eggplants?" —*Iona Knight*
Richland Center, Wisconsin

OUR FAMILY was picking strawberries, and my step-daughter ate some as she helped pick.

After a while, she came up to me, pointed to her stomach and said with the cutest giggle, "I brought my own bucket."

—*Dana Phillips*
Clarksville, Arkansas

I WAS planting a climbing variety of lima beans. As I set up the poles, I explained to our young son, "We'll plant the seeds so the plants can grow up the stakes."

To which he responded, "Can I help plant these *cli-ma* beans?" —*Ila Bradle*
Secor, Illinois

MY 3-year-old grandson was very excited about some tomato plants his mother had set out.

One day while I was vis-iting, he just had to show me the garden. When he saw the green tomatoes that were beginning to appear, he exclaimed, "We're going to have to paint them red!" —*Pat Pruitt* *Travelers Rest, South Carolina*

WHEN Christian, my 3-year-old grandson, visited, he went with me to the garden to harvest seeds from my four o'clock flowers.

When we had our bag almost full, Christian looked into the bag and said, "Grandma, are the clock seeds ticking?" —*Malolah Fullbright* *Amarillo, Texas*

MY 2-year-old "helped" me plant early peas one spring morning, and then stayed outside to play. When he came into the house later for lunch, he announced, "Mom, my shoes are full of garden!" —*Rosie Swarey* *Meyersdale, Pennsylvania*

DURING a summer visit to my house, my 3-year-old niece went with me to the garden. As we passed my rows of flowers, I asked, "Does your mommy (an avid vegetable grower) have flowers in her garden, too?"

She thought a moment and replied, "No...all she grows is dinner!" —*Christine Rausch* *Marysville, Ohio*

NOT QUITE RIPE. "Granddaughter Michaela wanted to taste the first tomato of the season, but it wasn't what she expected," says Norma Miller of Toledo, Ohio.

HAPPY HOLSTEIN. "Our niece Stacy and 'Cinnamon' the calf were smitten with each other," says Kathy Adams, Phelps, N.Y.